T0135703

Roland Petrasch, Florian Fieber, Mirjana Ivanovic, Zoran Budimac, Dragan Macos, Nils Mitoussis (Eds.)

Model Driven Software Engineering - Transformations and Tools

3rd Workshop of the Special Interest Group „Model-Driven Software Engineering" 2008, Berlin, Germany (MDSE 08)

Bibliografische Information der Deutschen Nationalbibliothek

Die Deutsche Nationalbibliothek verzeichnet diese Publikation in der
Deutschen Nationalbibliografie; detaillierte bibliografische Daten sind
im Internet über http://dnb.d-nb.de abrufbar.

ISBN 978-3-8325-2187-5

Logos Verlag Berlin GmbH
Comeniushof, Gubener Str. 47,
10243 Berlin
Tel.: +49 030 42 85 10 90
Fax: +49 030 42 85 10 92
INTERNET: http://www.logos-verlag.de

Foreword

Approaches for MDSE (Model-Driven Software Engineering) like OMG's Model Driven Architecture (MDA) focus on the separation of the specification of the system from its implementation on a particular platform. The MDA pattern with its platform-independent model (PIM) and the transformation to one or more platform-specific models (PSMs) is well known. However, in practice many different methodologies and tools are used to take advantage of model driven software development. Some tools are using MOF-compliant languages such as UML for modeling and a subset of MOF-QVT implementation for transformations while others are using proprietary languages. The goal of this workshop is to bring together people working on MDSE techniques and tools, and applying them on web applications, enterprise information systems or embedded systems, so that they can exchange their experience, create new ideas, evaluate and improve MDSE and spread its use. This year, we take a closer look at transformations, e.g. model-to-model and model-to-text transformations, transformation languages and transformation specification. We also focus on the human factor, e.g. qualification of software engineers for MDA.

Information about the Special Interest Group can be found on www.sig-mdse.org

Roland Petrasch, Florian Fieber, Mirjana Ivanovic, Zoran Budimac, Dragan Macos, Nils Mitoussis

Berlin, December 2008

3

Committees

Chairs
Roland Petrasch (Chair) and Dragan Macos (Co-Chair)
TFH, Univ. of Applied Sciences Berlin,
Department of Informatics and Media
Germany
petrasch@tfh-berlin.de, dmacos@tfh-berlin.de

Mirjana Ivanovic (Co-Chair), Zoran Budimac (Co-Chair)
University of Novi Sad
Faculty of Science
Department of Mathematics and Informatics
Serbia
mira@im.ns.ac.yu, zjb@im.ns.ac.yu

Workshop Program Committee
Silvia Abrahao, Universidad Politécnica de Valencia, Spain
Costin Badica, University of Craiova, Romania
Steffen Becker, FZI Forschungszentrum Informatik, Karlsruhe, Germany
Zoran Budimac, University of Novi Sad, Serbia
Matthias Bohlen, Germany
Kasidit Chancio, Thammasat University, Bangkok, Thailand
Florian Fieber, qme Software, Berlin, Germany
Peter Forbrig, Universität Rostock
Zdenek Havlice, Technical University of Kosice, Slovakia
Zoltán Horváth, Eötvös Loránd University, Hungary
Mirjana Ivanovic, University of Novi Sad, Serbia
Petros Kefalas, CITY College, Thessaloniki, Greece
Dragan Macos, TFH - University of Applied Sciences, Berlin, Germany
Jason Mansell, Fundación European Software Institute, Spain
Slavko Marić, University of Banja Luka, Bosnia and Herzegovina
Dragan Milicev, University of Belgrade, Serbia
Nils Mitoussis, TFH - University of Applied Sciences, Berlin, Germany
Wolfgang Neuhaus, Itemis AG, Lünen
Marek Paralic, Technical University of Kosice, Slovakia
Roland Petrasch, TFH - University of Applied Sciences, Berlin, Germany
Songsak Rongviriyapanich, Thammasat University, Bangkok, Thailand
Stanimir Stoyanov, University of Plovdiv, Bulgaria
Maik Thränert, University of Leipzig, Germany
Olegas Vasilecas, Vilnius Gediminas Technical University, Lithuania
Hussein Zedan, De Montfort University, Leicester, UK
Frank Zimmermann, Nordakademie, Germany

Organization Committee
Mirjana Ivanovic, University of Novi Sad, Serbia
Nils Mitoussis, TFH - University of Applied Sciences, Berlin, Germany (Chair)
Roland Petrasch, TFH - University of Applied Sciences, Berlin, Germany
Zoran Putnik, University of Novi Sad, Serbia

Venue / Workshop Location

qme Software, Gustav-Meyer-Allee 25, 13355 Berlin, Germany

Sponsors

The chairs and committee member send their thanks to the sponsors for the help.

 Special Interest Group
Model Driven Software En-
gineering

 qme Software, Berlin, Germany

 Projektron GmbH, Berlin, Germany

 Transentis management consulting GmbH, Austria

 Itemis AG, Lünen, Germany

 Thammasat University, Bangkok, Thailand

5

University Novi Sad, Serbia

TFH Berlin, University of Applied Sciences, Germany

Contents

Refinement Transformation Support for QVT Relational Transformations 1
Thomas Goldschmidt, Guido Wachsmuth

MDA Transformation Languages – Exploration and Comparison of Capability and Quality Characteristics 15
Nils Mitoussis, Dragan Macos

Modelling Graphical User Interfaces for embedded Systems 29
Georg Dummer, Thomas Schuster, Dennis Ritter, Klaus D. Müller-Glaser

User Interfaces from Task Models 43
Peter Forbrig, Daniel Reichart, Andreas Wolff

HCI Patterns in the Context of Model Driven Development™ for Interactive Systems 61
Roland Petrasch, Max Bureck

On-the-fly MDA application modelling using Executable and Translatable UML 77
Otto Zeleznik, Zdenek Havlice

An Application of the MDSE Principles in IIS*Case 85
Ivan Lukovic, Sonja Ristic, Slavica Aleksic, Aleksandar Popovic

GenGMF: Efficient editor development for large meta models using the Graphical Modeling Framework 97
Enrico Schnepel

Modelling Behaviour by Activity Diagrams and Complete Code Generation 105
Erwin Neuhardt

Model-Driven Architecture for an Interactive Ajax Mapping Platform . . 117
Tobias Weidemann, Tobias Hüttner, Frank Hanisch

Customizing the JET2 Template Engine 133
Marc-Florian Wendland

7

Refinement Transformation Support for QVT Relational Transformations

Thomas Goldschmidt

FZI Research Center for Information Technology

Haid-und-Neu-Str. 10-14

76131 Karlsruhe

Germany

goldschmidt@fzi.de

Guido Wachsmuth

Humboldt-Universität zu Berlin

Unter den Linden 6

10099 Berlin

Germany

guwac@gk-metrik.de

Abstract

Model transformations are a central concept in Model-driven Engineering. Model transformations are defined in model transformation languages. This paper addresses QVT Relations, a high-level declarative model transformation language standardised by the Object Management Group. QVT Relations lacks support for default copy rules. Thus, transformation developers need to define copy rules explicitly. Particular for refinement transformations which copy large parts of a model, this is a tremendous task. In this paper, we propose generic patterns for copy rules in QVT Relations. Based on these patterns, we provide a higher-roder transformation to generate copy rules for a given metamodel. Finally, we explore several ways to derive a refinement transformation from a generated copy transformation.

1. Introduction

Model transformations. In Model-driven Engineering, model transformations are a central concept. They are used to translate source models to target models, e.g. platform-independent models into platform-specific ones. Furthermore, model transformations can be instrumented to translate models into text, e.g. in an executable language like Java [1]. With Query/View/Transformation (QVT) [2], the Object Management Group provides a standard for model-to-model transformations. Actually, QVT defines three model transformation languages: *QVT Relations* and *QVT Core* are declarative languages at two different levels of abstraction. The *QVT Operational Mappings* lan-

1

guage is an imperative language. In this paper, we focus on QVT Relations, the high-level declarative language.

One can distinguish two kinds of model-to-model transformations: *Exogenous transformations* translate models expressed in a certain source language into models expressed in a different target language. For *endogenous transformations*, source and target models are expressed in the same language. The target model can be either derived by changing the input model *in-place* or by creating an entire new model.

Model refinements. Often, the target model of a transformation is simply a *refinement* of the source model, that is, the transformation preserves large parts of the source. Refinements might be either endogenous, e.g. an optimisation, or exogenous, e.g. migration to a new language version. Though in-place transformations are particular useful to describe refinements in a compact way, there are several reasons to prefer the creation of a new model: First, the source model is preserved. Second, traces between the source and target model become explicit. Finally, with QVT Relations, exogenous refinements need to be described explicitly since in-place transformations are restricted to endogenous transformations.

A transformation realising a refinement needs to copy large parts of a model. Since QVT Relations does not support default copies, a refinement definition needs to specify copies explicitly. In this paper, we investigate copies in QVT Relations. First, we propose generic patterns for copy rules. Second, we provide a way to generate the definition of a copy transformation for a given metamodel. The generation is specified as a higher-order transformation. Finally, we explore several ways to derive a refinement from a generated copy transformation.

Structure of the paper. In Section 2, we discuss related work. In Section 3, we examine generic patterns in copy rules. In Section 4, we present a higher-order transformation for the generation of copy transformations. In Section 5, we discuss the derivation of refinement transformations out of generated copy transformations. The paper is concluded in Section 6.

2. Related Work

In contrast to QVT Relations, QVT Operational Mappings provide a *deep copy* operation that can be used within imperative mapping rules. This operation creates a copy of a given substructure. However, it is not possible to specify exceptions for elements that occur within the substructure that is copied. Therefore, this approach is only partially useful for a refinement transformation.

The Atlas Transformation Language (ATL) [3] supports a special mode that allows the transformation programmer to specify that a transformation should be run as a refinement transformation. This means that all elements are copied by default whilst those elements that are matched by transformation rules within the actual transformation are not. Those elements are instead treated as specified by the given transformation rules.

Another model transformation approach is the Triple Graph Grammar (TGG) [5] approach. Within this approach the standard execution mechanism is described as being an in-place transformation where transformation rules are applied as long as there are

2

rules that still match patterns within the model. So, TGGs can naturally be used for endogenous, in-place transformations and do not need special support for copy rules.

3. Generic Patterns for Copy Rules

In this section, we will discuss generic patterns for copy rules. We illustrate these patterns by copy rules for Petri net models.

Example: Petri net models

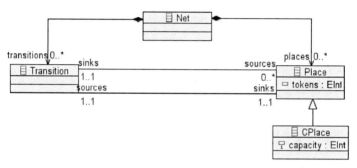

Figure 3.1: Example metamodel for Petri nets

Figure 3.1 shows a metamodel for Petri net models: A *Net* consists of *places* and *transitions*. A *Transition* has several places as *sources* and as *sinks*. In the same way, a *Place* has several transitions as *sources* and as *sinks*. Furthermore, a place is marked by an optional number of *tokens*. A *CPlace* is additionally constrained by a maximal capacity.

Copying Petri nets reveals several issues:

(i) Nets, places, and transitions need to be copied.

(ii) For places, we need to preserve their kind (*Place* vs. *CPlace*).

(iii) For places, we need to preserve the number of marking tokens. The same holds for capacities.

(iv) Links between nets, places, and transitions need to be copied.

Copying instances

The first two issues concern copies of metaclass instances. For a non-abstract metaclass, we define a *copy relation* to specify copies of its instances. In the source model, this relation simply matches an instance of the metaclass. In the target model, the relation enforces a corresponding instance of the same metaclass. Declaring the relation as top ensures that the relation is applied to every instance of the metamodel in the source model.

Listing 3.1 shows such a relation *copyNet* for the metaclass *Net*.

```
top relation copyNet {
    checkonly domain orig netO: Net {};
    enforce domain copy netC: Net {};
    where { copiedNet(netO, netC); }
}

relation copiedNet {
    checkonly domain orig netO: Net {};
    checkonly domain copy netC: Net {};
}
```

Listing 3.1 Copy and marker relations for metaclass Net.

In the *where* clause of this relation, another relation *copiedNet* is called with the original net and its copy as arguments. This *marker relation* is shown as well in Listing 3.1. Marker relations are non-top relations that simply match their arguments in the source and target model. We use such relations to indicate which elements have already been copied. Once an element is copied, we call the corresponding marker relation from the *where* clause.

```
top relation copyPlace {
    checkonly domain orig placeO: Place {};
    enforce domain copy placeC: Place {};
    when { not copiedCPlace(placeO, placeC); }
    where { copiedPlace(placeO, placeC); }
}
top relation copyCPlace {
    checkonly domain orig placeO: CPlace {};
    enforce domain copy placeC: CPlace {};
    where { copiedCPlace(placeO, placeC); }
}
relation copiedPlace {
    checkonly domain orig placeO: Place {};
    checkonly domain copy placeC: Place {};
}
relation copiedCPlace {
    checkonly domain orig placeO: Place {};
    checkonly domain copy placeC: Place {};
    where { copiedPlace(placeO, placeC); }
}
```

Listing 3.2 Copy and marker relations for metaclasses Place and CPlace.

Listing 3.2 shows the copy and marker relations for *Place* and *CPlace*. It illustrates

4

how marker relations for subclasses call the marker relations for their superclasses, that is, *copiedCPlace* calls *copiedPlace* from its *where* clause. This way, we can indicate that an instance was already copied by a more specific rule. The *when* clause of *copy-Place* ensures this. The relation is only executed, if *copiedCPlace* is never called for a given pair of places in the source and target model. To make this pattern work for any given class hierarchy, we need marker relations for abstract meta-classes as well.

Copying slots and links

The last two issues concern copies of slots and links. Both can be achieved in a similar way. To copy slots instantiating an attribute defined by a metaclass, we define a top relation for this attribute. In the source model, the relation matches an instance of the metaclass as well as the value stored in the slot corresponding to the attribute. In the target model, another instance of the metaclass is matched. The original value is copied to the corresponding slot in the target instance. The when clause of the relation needs to ensure that the target instance is a copy of the source instance by calling a marker relation. Listing 3.3 shows the copy relation for *Place.tokens*. Since the marker relation *copiedCPlace* calls *copiedPlace*, this relation will copy tokens slots for instances of *CPlace* as well.

```
top relation copyPlace_token {
    tokenO: Integer;
    checkonly domain orig placeO: Place { tokens = tokenO };
    enforce domain copy placeC: Place { tokens = tokenO };
    when { copiedPlace(placeO, placeC); }
}
```

Listing 3.3 Copy relation for attribute Place.tokens.

To copy links instantiating a reference between metaclasses, the pattern is quite similar. We define a top relation for the reference matching instances in the source and target model. In both models, the relation matches two instances connected by a link. The *when* clause ensures that instances in the target model are copies of the instances in the source model. Listing 3.4 shows the copy relations for *Place.sources* and *Place.sinks*.

```
top relation copyPlace_sources {
    checkonly domain orig placeO: Place {
        sources = transO: Transition {}
    };
    enforce domain copy placeC: Place {
        sources = transC: Transition {}
    };
    when {
        copiedPlace(placeO, placeC);
        copiedTransition(transO, transC);
    }
```

5

```
}

top relation copyPlace_sinks {
    checkonly domain orig placeO: Place {
        sinks = transO: Transition {}
    };
    enforce domain copy placeC: Place {
        sinks = transC: Transition {}
    };
    when {
        copiedPlace(placeO, placeC);
        copiedTransition(transO, transC);
    }
}
```

Listing 3.4 Copy relations for references Place.source and Place.sink.

For a pair of bidirectional references, only one copy relation for one of the references is needed.

4.   Generation of Copy Transformations

The patterns presented in Section 3 can be used to specify a copy transformation in QVT Relations for arbitrary Ecore metamodels. Obviously, these patters are that generic that we can generate a copy transformation directly and automatically from a given metamodel. In this section, we investigate a *higher-order transformation* for this purpose. This higher-order transformation is written in QVT Relations itself and captures the patterns discussed in the preceding section. It is based on the Ecore meta-meta-model, on the OCL standard library (for negation), and on the QVT Relations meta-model. After executing this higher-order transformation, a complete model of the copy transformation is available. This can then either directly be used in its abstract syntax or a simple pretty printer can be used to print it in its textual concrete syntax.

4.1. Overall Structure

The overall structure of the higher-order transformation is shown in Listing 4.1. Basically, the transformation works analogously to the patterns of Section 3. For each package in the metamodel, a copy transformation is generated (c.f. Package2Transformation). The name of this transformation is derived from the package name. The copy transformation declares two domains *source* and *target*, both typed by the metamodel package.

```
transformation emf2copyQVT (
    mm: ecore, oclstdlib:ecore, qvt: QVTRelation
) {
    top relation Package2Transformation {
```

```
        n:String;
        checkonly domain mm ePackage: EPackage { name = n };
        enforce domain qvt t: RelationalTransformation {
            name = 'Copy' + n,
            modelParameter = sourceMM: TypedModel {
                name = 'source',
                usedPackage = ePackage2: EPackage{}
            },
            modelParameter = targetMM: TypedModel {
                name = 'target',
                usedPackage = ePackage3: EPackage{}
            }
        };
        where { ePackage2 = ePackage; ePackage3 = ePackage; }
    }
    top relation Class2CopyRelation { ... }
    top relation Class2MarkerRelation { ... }
    top relation Attribute2CopyRelation { ... }
    top relation Reference2CopyRelation { ... }

    relation SubClass2MarkerCallInWhen { ... }
    relation SuperClass2MarkerCallInWhere { ... }
    relation MarkMappedVariables { ... }
}
```

Listing 4.1 Overall structure of the higher-order transformation emf2copyQVT.

The remaining relations of the higher-order transformation generate the relations of the copy transformation:

(i) For each non-abstract metaclass, a copy relation is generated (c.f. Class2CopyRelation).

(ii) For each subclass, a negated call to the corresponding marker relation is added to the *when* clause of a copy relation (c.f. SubClass2MarkerCallInWhen).

(iii) For each metaclass, a marker relation is generated (c.f. Class2MarkerRelation).

(iv) For each superclass, a call to the corresponding marker relation is added to the *where* clause of a marker relation (c.f. SuperClass2MarkerCallInWhere).

(v) For each attribute, a copy relation is generated (c.f. Attribute2CopyRelation).

(vi) For each relation, a copy relation is generated (c.f. Reference2CopyRelation).

We will discuss the details of the generation in the remainder of this section.

4.2. Generating copy relations from metaclasses

Listing 4.2 and Listing 4.3 show relations for the generation of copy relations from metaclasses. For each non-abstract metaclass within a metamodel package, a copy relation is created (c.f. Class2CopyRelation). The pattern for creating the relation looks very complicated due to the heavily nested abstract syntax. We omit some reoccurring

7

patterns, that is, for tVar and targetDom, which are quite similar to the patterns for sVar and sourceDom. During the creation, a *where* clause is generated that contains a RelationCallExp to call the corresponding marker relation.

```
top relation Class2CopyRelation {
    markerRel : QVTRelation::Relation;
    checkonly domain mm eClass: EClass {
        name = n : String{}, abstract = false
    };
    enforce domain qvt r: Relation {
        name = 'Copy' + n, isTopLevel = true,
        variable = sVar: Variable {
            name = n + '_source', eType = eClass
        },
        variable = tVar: Variable { ... },
        _domain = sourceDom: RelationDomain {
            pattern = sourcePattern: DomainPattern {
                templateExpression = sExpr: ObjectTemplateExp {
                    referredClass = eClass
                },
                bindsTo = sVar: Variable {}
            },
            rootVariable = sVar
        },
        _domain = targetDom: QVTRelation::RelationDomain { ... },
        _transformation = transfo: RelationalTransformation {},
        _where = callMarker: Pattern {
            predicate = p: Predicate {
                conditionExpression = a: RelationCallExp{
                    referredRelation = markerRel,
                    argument = supSourceVarExp: VariableExp{
                        referredVariable = sVar
                    },
                    argument = supTargetVarExp: VariableExp{
                        referredVariable = tVar
                    }
                }
            }
        },
        _when = whenP: Pattern {}
    };
    when {Package2Transformation(eClass.ePackage, transfo);
        Class2MarkerRelation(eClass, markerRel);
    }
    where { MarkMappedVariables(eClass, r, sVar, tVar, whenP); }
}
```

Listing 4.2 Generating a copy relation from a metaclass.

```
top relation SubClass2MarkerCallInWhen {
    checkonly domain mm subClass: EClass {
        eSuperTypes = supertype: EClass {}
    };
    checkonly domain oclstdlib stdlibPkg: EPackage {
        name = 'oclstdlib',
        eClassifiers = notOpContainer: EClass {
            eOperations = notOp: EOperation { name = 'not' }
        }
    };
    enforce domain qvt r: Relation {
        _when = whenP: Pattern {
            predicate = p: Predicate {
                conditionExpression = notC: OperationCallExp {
                    referredOperation = notOp,
                    argument = relCall: RelationCallExp { ... }
                }
            }
        }
    };
    when {
        Class2CopyRelation(supertype, r);
        MarkMappedVariables(supertype, r, sVar, tVar, whenP);
        Class2MarkerRelation(subClass, markerSubClass);
    }
}
```

Listing 4.3 Generating negated marker calls from subclasses.

The *when* clauses of copy relations are generated by a separate relation (c.f. SubClass2-MarkerCallInWhen). For each direct subclass, a negated RelationCallExp calling the marker relation of this subclass is generated. The pattern for this call is quite similar to the one for the *where* clause. Therefor, we ommit it.

4.3. Generating marker relations from metaclasses

Listing 4.4 shows relations for the generation of marker relations. Marker relations are generated for each metaclass including abstract ones (c.f. Class2MarkerRelation). The patterns for generating the source and target variables and domains are the same as for the generation of copy relations. We omit them for brevity. For each direct superclass, a call to the marker relation of this superclass is added to the *where* clause. Again, this is achieved by a separate relation (c.f. SuperClass2MarkerCallInWhere) similar to the one for negated calls in *when* clauses.

9

```
top relation Class2MarkerRelation {
    checkonly domain mm eClass: EClass { name = n : String{} };
    enforce domain qvt r: Relation {
        name = 'Mark' + n, isTopLevel = false,
        variable = sVar: Variable { ... },
        variable = tVar: Variable { ... },
        _domain = sourceDom: RelationDomain { ... },
        _domain = targetDom: RelationDomain { ... },
        _transformation = RelationalTransformation {}
    };
    when { Package2Transformation(eClass.ePackage, transfo); }
    where {
        eClass.eSuperTypes->forAll(st |
            SuperClass2MarkerCallInWhere(st, r, sVar, tVar)
        );
    }
}
```

Listing 4.4 Generating marker relations from metaclasses.

4.4. Generating copy relations from attributes and references

Finally, Listing 4.5 shows a relation for the generation of copy relations from attributes. This relation generates a copy relation for each attribute in the metamodel. An analogue relation (c.f. Reference2CopyRelation) is used to create copy relations for references. Again, we omit patterns already mentioned in other listings.

```
top relation Attribute2Relation {
    markerRel: Relation;
    checkonly domain mm eClass: EClass { name = cn: String {} };
    checkonly domain mm attribute: EAttribute {
        name = an : String{}, eType = at: EDataType{}
    };
    enforce domain qvt r: Relation {
        name = 'Copy' + cn + '_' + an, isTopLevel = true,
        variable = sVar: Variable { ... },
        variable = tVar: Variable { ... },
        variable = atVar: Variable {
            name = 'ref' + cn + '_' + an, eType = at
        },
        _domain = sourceDom: RelationDomain {
            pattern = sourcePattern: DomainPattern {
                templateExpression = sExpr: ObjectTemplateExp {
                    referredClass = eClass,
                    part = refTemplateS: PropertyTemplateItem {
                        referredProperty = attribute,
                        value = sAttributeExp: VariableExp {
```

```
                    referredVariable = refVar
                }
            }
        },
        bindsTo = sVar: Variable {}
    },
    rootVariable = sVar
},
_domain = targetDom: RelationDomain { ... },
_transformation = transfo: RelationalTransformation {},
_when = callMarker: Pattern { ... };

when {
    Package2Transformation(eClass.ePackage, transfo);
    Class2MarkerRelation(eClass, markerRel);
    eClass.eStructuralFeatures->includes(attribute);
}
}
```

Listing 4.5 Generating copy relations from attributes and references.

5. Writing Refinement Transformations

There are two possibilities to specify a refinement transformation based on a generated copy transformation. First, by writing a new transformation manually that overwrites specific rules of the generic copy transformation. The rules of the refinement transformation are then called instead of the overwritten ones within the copy transformation. This enables us to handle those parts of the model that should be treated other then a mere copy. Second, it could be possible to define a transformation that only contains the exception rules and then use a higher-order transformation to weave these rules into a generated copy transformation.

Manually Extended Transformation

According to the QVT Relations specification [2], it is possible to define *extension* transformations. Within an extension, it is possible to define rules that conditionally *override* rules from the extended transformation. However, the exact semantics of the override mechanism is not defined within the standard. For example, it is not mentioned if this conditional override means that for elements where the overriding pattern does not match the overridden rule is used instead or if the element is not matched at all. Furthermore, QVT Relations engines like mediniQVT [4] currently also do not support this feature. Nevertheless, we propose extension as a natural way to specify refinement transformations with help of a generated copy transformation.

The transformation developer has to make sure that only *complete* rules should be provided by the extension. *Complete* in this case means that for each manually specified refinement rule a complementary rule needs to be specified that matches all elements that are *not* matched by the refinement rule. Only then it can be ensured that all model ele-

11

ments not handled by the refinement rules are normally copied. An easy way to ensure this is to call the refinement transformation as well as the corresponding generic copy rule using an exclusive or within the *where* statement of a third rule that has the same source pattern as the copy rule.

Another problem with extension is that the user has to make sure that the corresponding marker relations are called within refinement rules. Otherwise all dependent generated copy rules will not execute. An example for this manual extension can be seen in listing 5.1.

```
transformation refinePN extends copyPN (orig: petri, copy: petri) {

    top relation refinedCopyNetCall overrides copyPN::copyNet{
        checkonly domain orig netO: Net {};
        enforce domain copy netC: Net {};
        where { if (refinedCopyNet(netO, netC)) then true
                else copyPN::copyNet(netO, netC) endif; }
    }
    relation refinedCopyNet {
        toks, newToks : Integer;
        checkonly domain orig netO: Net {
            p = refP : Place{token = toks}
        };
        enforce domain copy netC: Net {
            p = refP : Place{token = newToks}
        };
        when {toks = 0;}
        where { copyPN::copiedNet(netO, netC); }
    }
}
```

Listing 5.1 Using manual extension to refine the copy transformation

Automatic Weaving

The second possibility to create the desired refinement transformation is based on a transformation weaving technique. As depicted in figure 5.1 the rules that resemble the intended refinements are specified as standard QVT Relations transformation (c.f. $T(M_2M_2)$). As a next step, this transformation is tagged as being a refinement transformation. This tagging can, for instance, be done using either comments on the textual concrete syntax of the transformation or as a non-intrusive decorator model on the model (abstract syntax) of the transformation.

Figure 5.1 Automatic Weaving of Exception Rules

The tagged transformation is then transformed by a higher-order transformation (c.f. *HOT*). This transformation translates the refinement rules in a way that they conform to the expected calls of the marker relations (see Section 4). Furthermore, it generates copy rules (as defined in section 4) for those patterns that are not handled by the refinement. This step is based on the metamodel M_2 that is used as input and output parameter of the refinement transformation. As the refinement rules may only match a part of the elements that were normally matched by their corresponding copy rules, a similar construct has to be introduced as it is shown in section 5.1.

Using the tagging and weaving approach the transformation developer does not need to care about ensuring the consistency of the refinement rules with the generated copy rules. However, as the developer does not necessarily see the generated transformation which is executed, debugging is more complicated in this case. Additional support for tracing the debug information within the generated transformation back to the original transformation would be required. We prefer to use model-to-model over model-to-text transformations for the higher-order transformations as tracing is included in most of such engines. These traces can then easily be used during debugging to easily navigate from the generated, actually debugged transformation elements to their original, manually specified elements.

A similar refinement technique is described in [6] called *superimposition*. The superimposing transformation loosely overrides rules of the superimposed transformation with the same name. A higher-order transformation is then used to merge both transformations into a third one. A similar approach is used here when weaving the explicit refinement rules with generated copy rules. However, in this case there is no explicit superimposed transformation, as the copy rules (which would be superimposed by the refinement rules) are also generated during the weaving process and do not exist before.

6. Concluding Remarks

We presented an approach that allows transformation developers to circumvent the lack of default copy rules within QVT Relations. We presented generic patterns for copying instances, slots, and links. Based on these patterns, we provided a higher-order transformation for generating a copy transformation from a metamodel. The higher-order transformation is written in QVT Relations. Finally, we proposed two different possibilities on how the approach can be integrated into the development of refinement transformations. Future work will address the support for exogenous refinement transformations.

References

1. Czarnecki, K., Helsen, S.: Classification of model transformation approaches. OOPSLA (2003)

2. Object Management Group: Meta Object Facility (MOF) 2.0 Query/View/Transformation (QVT) http://www.omg.org/docs/formal/08-04-03.pdf.

3. Mens, T, Gorp, P.V.: A taxonomy of model transformation. GraMoT (2005).

4. Jouault, F., Allilaire, F., Bézivin, J., Kurtev, I.: ATL: A model transformation tool.

Science of Computer Programming, Special Issue on Second issue of experimental software and toolkits (EST) 72(1-2) (2008) 31–39

5. ikv++: medini QVT. http://www.ikv.de/ Last retrieved 2008-10-30.

6. Schürr, A.: Specification of Graph Translators with Triple Graph Grammars. In G. Tinhofer, editor, WG'94 20th Int. Workshop on Graph-Theoretic Concepts in Computer Science, volume 903 of Lecture Notes in Computer Science (LNCS), pages 151–163,Heidelberg, 1994. Springer Verlag.

7. Wagelaar, D.: Composition Techniques for Rule-Based Model Transformation Languages, 1st International Conference on Model Transformation - Theory and Practice of Model Transformations, volume 5063 of Lecture Notes in Computer Science (LNCS), pages 152-167, Heidelberg, 2008. Springer Verlag.

MDA Transformation Languages – Exploration and Comparison of Capability and Quality Characteristics

Nils Mitoussis, Dragan Macos
TFH Berlin – University of Applied Sciences
Department of Informatics and Media
Luxemburger Str. 10, D-13353 Berlin
{mitoussis | dmacos}@tfh-berlin.de

1 Abstract

Model transformation is a key aspect for the OMG's Model-driven Architecture (MDA). This paper focuses on exploration and comparison of different transformation languages for model-to-model-transformations in general, based on the specific languages QVT Relations, QVT Operational Mappings, ATL and Xtend. Their capability and quality characteristics are evaluated concerning maintainability, readability and reusability of the transformation definition. The exploration also involves relevant design principles of programming languages, in particular possibilities of abstraction. Based on these explorations, a method for comparison is presented including a visual representation. Finally, the four languages are compared and evaluated accordingly and recommendations for future implementations of transformation languages are given.

2 Introduction

The OMG's MDA Guide refers to additional specifications for model transformation languages [OMG03, p. 3-6]. The OMG finally approved the final specification of the MOF 2.0 QVT (Query / View / Transformation) standard in 2007 [QVT07], leading to a version 1.0 in 2008 [QVT08]. In the meantime, several other languages has been developed and used in practice, some of them as a response to the MOF 2.0 QVT Request for Proposals (RFP). Because they differ significantly in their concepts, further studies are valuable for language selection and language development.

In order to ensure an automated transformation execution, this paper addresses formal transformation languages and introduces methods and principles for a comparison and evaluation of transformation language features. A specific overview of results and discussion is given for the languages QVT Relations, QVT Operational Mappings, ATL and Xtend, leading to concluding remarks for further language development.

15

3 Related Work

A detailed classification of transformation approaches is presented by Czarnecki and Helsen in [CH03] and a revised work as a feature-based survey of model transformation approaches in [CH06].

Lawley et al. describe features supporting re-use and maintainability for their model transformation language Tefkat in [LDGR04]. Tefkat was a language proposed by DSTC in response to the OMG's MOF 2.0 QVT Request for Proposals (RFP), but differs significantly from the QVT Final Adopted Specification [QVT07].

Gardner et al. reviewed and compared early submissions to the OMG's MOF 2.0 QVT RFP in [GGKH03]. They discuss highlights and present recommendations for the final standard. A simple visual presentation is given for comparing characteristics of the different languages. The presentation spreads over several views, one for each of two features.

4 Classification Scheme

The following scheme was created as a result of a detailed exploration for QVT Relations, QVT Operational Mappings [QVT07], ATL [ATL06] and Xtend [EFH+07]. Maintainability, readability and reusability should be central aspects, but current quality models or taxonomies such as in [FGR+97], [Boe+78] or ISO 9126 hardly lead to very specific language features. We therefore deduced from that models specific features, e. g. focusing on the design principles abstraction, encapsulation, automation, simplicity, orthogonality, regularity and extensibility, as well as error prevention and error handling. The exploration was supported by a practical transformation project realized both with ATL and Xtend separately.

Originally, the exploration also involved the model-to-text transformation languages MOFScript and Xpand, which were used in addition to the model-to-model languages in the practical project.

4.1 Characteristics Common for Several Languages

The exploration showed that several languages in the same language family share a common type system and a common expression language. They are used by the particular language and are extended in some cases. The part of the scheme concerning type system and expression language is therefore treated separately in section A. This separation later allows a comparison mostly independent from the concrete languages. Where appropriate, some parts are following [CH06].

A. Type System and Expression Language

A.1 Foundation – Underlying specification.

A.2 Typing – Strength of typing, classification in *strong* or *weak* typing.

A.3 Types – Predefined primitive types, types for lists and compositions, types for undefined values and possibilities for user-defined types.

A.4 **Polymorphism** – inheritance, multiple inheritance, overloading, parametric types.

A.5 **Type Checking** – *static* or *dynamic* type checking [CW85, p. 5].

4.2 Language-specific characteristics

The relevant language specific characteristics are classified as follows.

B. Basic Features

B.1 **Language paradigm** – *declarative*, *imperative* or *hybrid*, when declarative and imperative are combined.

B.2 **Directionality and Cardinality** – Possible execution directions of the transformation, *unidirectional* or *bidirectional* and the number of possible source and target models.

B.3 **Language Syntax** – type of the transformation description formalism, e. g. *textual* or *graphical* as well as the *number of keywords* as an indicator for the language *simplicity* and *orthogonality* (if the keyword number is combined with language expressiveness).

B.4 **Types** – basic constructs of the language type system (see A.). Main typing properties are *strong* or *weak, implicit or explicit* as well as *static* or *dynamic* type checking.

B.5 **Error handling** – error handling mechanisms e. g. exceptions.

B.6 **Documentation** – Outline and actuality of the language documentation with regard to language specification and implementation: *very low, low, medium, high, very high*.

B.7 **Tools support** – available implementations (see G.).

C. Transformation rules

C.1 **Rule Identifier** – Rule identifier as language construct.

C.2 **Rule Parameterisation** – The possibility of rule saturation with control flow parameters, generic rules, type variables, higher-order rules, as well as possibility to use the mentioned concepts as return values.

C.3 **Variables** – Global and local variables (e. g. in transformation rules), referential transparency.

C.4 **Patterns** – Pattern matching as possibility to define control flow sequences.

C.5 **Syntactic Separation** – Separation of different domains.

C.6 **Creation of Model Elements** – Mechanisms for explicit or (automatic) implicit creation of model elements.

C.7 **Helper functions and temporary data structures** – Helper functions for model navigation. Data structures for dumping temporary model data.

C.8 Repeating source elements – handling possibility for repeating source elements in particular at cyclic dependencies.

C.9 Extended programming language concepts – Reflection, aspect oriented programming.

C.10 Extensibility for external languages – Possibility of definitions of foreign functions in other languages with the goal to extend the transformation definition mechanism.

C.11 Specifics – Features with positive or negative impacts on modelling principles and appropriate capability and quality characteristics.

D. Rule Organization

D.1 Grouping of Rules – For separation of concerns, possibilities for structuring and modularization of rules into groups are needed, like units or modules. Especially *imports* for adding separated rules, *inheritance* for a more sophisticated combination of modules, and aspects of *encapsulation*.

D.2 Polymorphism – Possibilities for polymorphic units, for example *inheritance, overloading* or *overriding*.

D.3 Rule Combination – Rules may be combined by partly overriding, or using dedicated language constructs.

E. Rule Application Control

E.1 Form, Selection and Matching – Form and selection of a rule can be *implicit* or *explicit*, and may be completed by a *matching mechanism* for source elements as a selection criterion.

E.2 Organisational Structure – Rule execution may be identifiable oriented at *source* or *target model*.

E.3 Coupling – Coupling of rules may be *loose* or *tight*. Explicitly called rules are tight coupled, whereas implicitly called rules are loose coupled, e. g. by matching of source elements.

E.4 Phasing – Structuring of the transformation execution in several phases [CH06, p. 632], may affect the understandability of the process.

F. Generation and Traceability

F.1 Creation und Update – Possibilities of creating and manually updating models or textual artefacts. In-place updates are used for modifying a single model, which is both source and target. Incremental updates allow for partial modifications dependent on changes in a model.

F.2 Protection of manual changes – Manual changes in a target model require a mechanism of protection, because they would be overwritten in a second generation run.

F.3   Traceability – F.1 and F.2 partly require special trace information for tracing changes back. These information can be collected *implicitly* or *explicitly* and stored with the concerning artefact or separately.

G. Tool Support

G.1   Implementation – Development state and progress as well as licence of use.

G.2   Code Editor – Platform and functionality, e. g. syntax highlighting, code completion, even including meta-model elements, and possibilities of refactoring.

G.3   Execution and Debugging – How transformations are executed and in which way they can be controlled in a development environment. Furthermore possibilities for debugging like breakpoints, execution step by step, navigation within code or evaluation of variables.

G.4   Frameworks – Frameworks, in which the transformation language is integrated.

We explored the four languages in detail according to this scheme. A lot of information was retrieved from the specification or documentation, but some information could only be retrieved by analyzing the behaviour of the current implementation. A structured presentation of the detailed results is not given in this paper due to space limitations, but the results are reflected in the later visual comparison.

5   Visual Representation

The comparison of transformation languages appears to be easier in overview, if a visual representation of main characteristics can be presented. For this purpose, a *kiviat chart* is used with several characteristics assigned to the axes.

5.1   Selection and Reduction to Main Characteristics

First of all, the main language paradigm is specified by the ability to formulate **(1) declarative rules** and **(2) imperative rules**. Other key features of the language are **(3) execution direction** (bi- or unidirectional) as well as **(4) input cardinality** and **(5) output cardinality**. The cardinality is differentiated between a single model, a fixed number and an arbitrary number of models.

For the following quality-related characteristics, ratio scales were created for abstracting from the specific language features. Every feature is awarded a single point, normalizing the scale by the maximum of possible points.

(6) Simplicity reflects the number of keywords used by the language. **(7) Automation** describes whether elements can be created implicitly, repeating source elements are handled automatically, rules are selected implicitly, sources matched implicitly and traces created implicitly. **(8) Abstraction** includes if the language integrates several polymorphic type system features, generic rules, higher order rules, reflection, aspect-oriented programming (AOP), grouping of rules and polymorphic rules.

19

Another relevant issue is **(9) error handling**, which involves a message output, exceptions if an imperative paradigm is used, and a differentiation of undefined values (void, invalid) is implemented if a declarative paradigm is used. At the **(10) generation process**, features for model creation, model update, in-place update, incremental update are regarded, as well as protection capabilities for manual changes und support for traceability. In practice, the **(11) tool support** is relevant to the language usage. This includes an existing implementation, whether the implementation is advanced, several code editor features, execution in an IDE and debugging features. For effective usage of all features, extent and actuality of the **(12) documentation** are important.

5.2 Language metrics

The main characteristics are represented in a metric system by measurement in scales as follows.

1. **Declarative Rules** – references B.1
    Ordinal level of measurement, values are *yes* or *no*.
2. **Imperative Rules** – references B.1
    Ordinal level of measurement, values are *yes* or *no*.
3. **Execution Direction** – references B.2
    Ordinal level of measurement, values are *uni-* or *bidirectional.*
4. **Input Cardinality** – references B.1
    Ordinal level of measurement, values are *1, fixed number* or *arbitrary (N).*
5. **Output Cardinality** – references B.1
    Ordinal level of measurement, values are *1, fixed number* or *arbitrary (M).*
6. **Simplicity** – references B.3
    Ratio level of measurement, range 0..1, value is calculated as 1 – (maximum amount of keywords in comparison / language amount of keywords).
7. **Automation** – references C.6, C.8, E.1, F.3
    Ratio level of measurement, range 0..5, the points are accumulated.
    +1 implicit creation of elements (C.6)
    +1 automatic handling of repeated source elements (C.8)
    +1 implicit rule selection (E.1)
    +1 implicit source matching (E.1)
    +1 implicit creation of traces (F.3)
8. **Abstraction** – references A.4, C.2, C.9, D
    Ratio level of measurement, range 0..13, the points are accumulated.
    +1(*4) for each feature of a polymorphic type system (A.4)
    +1 generic rules (C.2)
    +1 higher-order rules (C.2)
    +1 reflection (C.9)
    +1 aspect-oriented programming (C.9)
    +1(*3) for each feature in grouping of rules (D.1)
    +1(*2) for each type in polymorphism (D.2)
9. **Error Handling** – references B.5, A.3

20

Ratio level of measurement, range 0..2 or 0..3, the points are accumulated.
+1 output of messages (B.5)
+1 exceptions (only imperative) (B.5)
+1 differentiation of undefined values in *void* and *invalid*, (only declarative) (A.3)

10. **Generation** – references F
Ratio level of measurement, range 0..6, the points are accumulated.
+1(*4) for each F.1 feature: model creation, model update, in-place update, incremental update
+1 protection of manual changes (F.2)
+1 support for traceability (F.3)

11. **Tool Support** – references B.7, G
Ratio level of measurement, range 0..12, the points are accumulated.
+1 availability of an implementation (G.1)
+1 advanced level of implementation development (G.1)
+1 code-editor (G.2)
+1(*4) for each additional code-editor feature (G.2)
+1 execution and control within an integrated development environment (G.3)
+1 explicit support for debugging (G.3)
+1(*4) for each additional debugging feature (G.3)

12. **Documentation** – references B.6
Ratio level of measurement, range 0..8. Extent and actuality in (B.6) are each rated in a range of 0..4 (*very low, low, medium, high, very high*)

All ratio levels of measurement can be normalized to a range of 0 to 100 percent, where 100 percent represents the maximum possible score. This eases the graphical representation.

6 Comparison

Visual Comparison

The languages QVT Relations, QVT Operational Mappings, ATL and Xtend are in the following visually presented according to the introduced evaluation and presentation method. Figures 1-4 show the corresponding diagrams.

The compact visualization gives a brief overview on the earlier defined main characteristics. Besides of the value for each characteristic and their graphical emphasis, the graphic can be seen as a whole in outline and surface. The arrangement of axes follows only a very loose relation between adjacent characteristics. Therefore, the interpretation of surface and outline is limited.

In general, a large and uniform surface indicates a rich-featured language and a high diversification of characteristics. A more scattered outline indicates a less diversified character, which may be the case for a more specialized language.

A simple visual overview comparison can be performed by putting multiple diagrams side by side. This is done in Figure 5.

Discussion of Specific Languages

Declarative Rules allow a more abstract definition and a more automated transformation. The transformation definition in source code is expected to be more compact and precise, which may prevent errors. On the other hand, understandability and readability depends on the abilities of the developer in the specific language. The imperative language paradigm is more common to programmers and therefore often easier to get started with.

QVT Relations (Figure 1) has a purely declarative style and the most complete set of generation features. QVT Operational Mappings (Figure 2) is only imperative but has a very high amount of imperative constructs and a high keyword count. The language has a high expressiveness which is useful in complex transformation scenarios but comes at the cost of simplicity. In QVT, Operational Mappings may be used as an addition in the Relations language [QVT07, p. 45], but this may reduce the capabilities of pure QVT Relations [QVT07, p. 11]. Therefore, the two languages are regarded separately.

ATL (Figure 3) is the only language in review that supports a hybrid paradigm including both imperative and declarative elements in a single language specification. ATL is the most diversified language and supports the highest automation. It allows for an arbitrary amount of input and output models. Other characteristics are average.

Xtend (Figure 4) is a pure declarative language with a manageable set of language constructs, but yet they are not very specific to model transformation. The declarative constructs in ATL and QVT Relations are in contrast more specific to model transformation, especially with syntactic separation for different domains. In ATL this is implemented very descriptive with from- and to-statements. QVT Relation omits any references to execution direction, which allows it to be the only language capable of bi-directional transformations.

Only ATL supports an implicit calling of rules with specific constraints for the source elements. This reduces coupling, but these implicitly called rules are limited in flexibility because they can not be used with parameters. In Xtend, rules can be overloaded supporting all dynamic parameter types for implicit rule selection, but no other constraints can be defined.

Elements can be created implicitly in all evaluated languages, but the languages differ in handling repeating source elements in cyclic graph scenarios. The QVT specification makes arrangements for a manual handling, whereas ATL and Xtend can treat this automatically which seems to be more appropriate.

The languages are all based on or at least oriented on the type system and the expression language defined by OCL. According to the OCL standard, they are all strongly typed and type checking should happen statically. But the ATL implementation yet only supports dynamic type checking. The languages all have slight divergences to the OCL standard in its different versions.

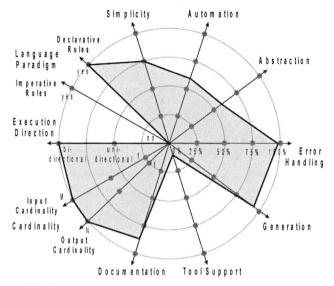

Figure 1: QVT Relations

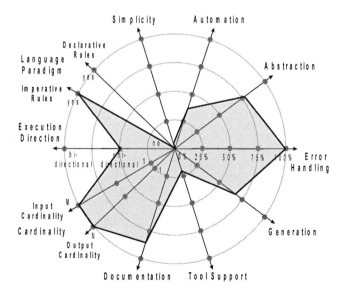

Figure 2: QVT Operational Mappings

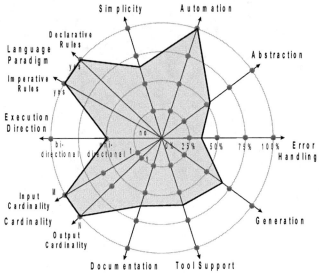

Figure 3: ATL

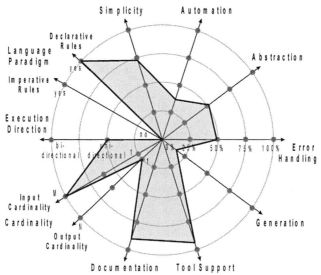

Figure 4: Xtend

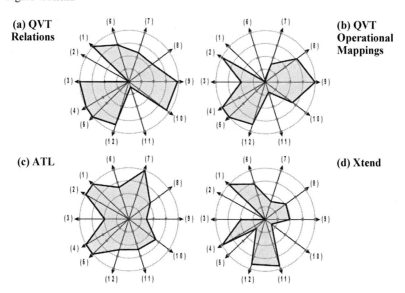

(a) QVT Relations

(b) QVT Operational Mappings

(c) ATL

(d) Xtend

Figure 5: Overview comparison of shapes and surfaces

The overview comparison in Figure 5 shows that ATL is likely to be the most diversified language with a very high automation. In contrast to ATL, other languages have higher peaks at specific other characteristics, so they are expected to be more powerful in these aspects. The importance of one characteristic or subsidiary feature over another in practice will depend on the needs of an individual project.

7 Conclusion

In our paper we evaluated four transformation languages: QVT Relations, QVT Operational Mappings, ATL and Xtend. We selected 12 metrics to compare the language characteristics. The languages' comparison is shown in Chapter 5.

QVT Relations allow very powerful generation features with its declarative style. QVT Operational Mappings has a comprehensive amount of imperative constructs. Relations can be complemented by Operational Mappings, but this reduces the capabilities of Relations. Further work on the impact of combining the QVT languages would be of interest.

ATL is the most diversified language and supports the highest automation. It matured in practice and shares some roots with the separate and more theoretically matured QVT final specification. Xtend is a pure declarative language with a manageable set of language constructs, but yet not very specific to model transformation.

Because of these differences, MDA Tools should support transformation languages in a modularized fashion so that they can be replaced or combined.

All chosen languages or language families allow at least for a declarative or hybrid (declarative and imperative) style for defining transformations. The main goal of further language development is establishing type safe and expressive language paradigms for defining transformations which is in other words programming an MDA generator. According to this goal, from our point of view, the implementation of following language aspects have to be investigated:

1. Non-strict Semantics: The main approach for implementing non-strict semantics is lazy evaluation. Declarative languages with lazy evaluation allow the manipulation of infinite data structures which implicates additional convenience in manipulation of model syntax threes.

2. Pattern Matching: Some of languages provide pattern matching to define the control flow of programs. We suggest the investigation of pattern matching implementation at languages without this strategy to allow comfortable syntax three analysis of models.

3. Higher-Order Functions: We believe, the higher-order functions allow the handling of syntax threes on a higher abstraction level. It reduces the generator programming effort.

4. Type Variables: Languages with type variables make generic manipulations of model threes possible.

5. Partial Evaluation: Constant results of transformation language Terms have to be

boxed in pre-evaluated representation of model syntax three to allow high-performance transformation execution.

8 References

[ATL06]   ATLAS Group: *ATL: Atlas Transformation Language – User Manual, Version 0.7*. February 2006 / March 21, 2006. http://www.eclipse.org/m2m/atl/doc/ATL_User_Manual%5Bv0.7 ⏎ %5D.pdf (visited October 4, 2007)

[Boe+78]   Boehm, B. W.; Brown, J. R.; Kaspar, H.; Lipow, M.; Macleod, G. J.; Merrit, M. J.: *Characteristics of Software Quality*. North-Holland, 1978.

[CH03]   Czarnecki, K.; Helsen, S.: *Classification of Transformation Approaches*. In: Proceedings of the 18th International Conference, OOPSLA'2003, Workshop on Generative Techniques in the context of Model Driven Architecture, Anaheim, California, USA, October 2003.

[CH06]   Czarnecki, K.; Helsen, S.: *Feature-based survey of model transformation approaches*. In: *IBM Systems Journal*, Vol. 45, No. 3, 2006, p. 621-645

[CW85]   Cardelli, L.; Wegner, P.: *On Understanding Types, Data Abstraction, and Polymorphism*. In: ACM Computing Surveys, Volume 17, No. 4, p. 471-522, December 1985.

[EFH+07]   Efftinge, S.; Friese, P.; Haase, A.; Kadura, C.; Kolb, B.; Moroff, D.; Thoms, K.; Völter, M.: *openArchitectureWare User Guide Version 4.2* September 15, 2007. http://www.eclipse.org/gmt/oaw/doc/4.2/ ⏎ openArchitectureWare-42-reference.pdf (visited October 21, 2007)

[FGR+97]   Foreman, J.; Gross, J.; Rosenstein, R.; Fisher, D.; Brune, K.: *C4 Software Technology Reference Guide – A Prototype. CMU/SEI-97-HB-001.* Software Engineering Institute, Carnegie Mellon University, Pittsburgh, PA, USA, 1997. http://www.sei.cmu.edu/pub/documents/97.reports/pdf/97hb001.pdf (visited December 8, 2007)

[GGKH03]   Gardner, T.; Griffin, C.; Koehler, J.; Hauser, R.: *A review of OMG MOF 2.0 Query / Views / Transformations Submissions and Recommendations towards the final Standard*. July 21, 2003. In: Evans, A.; Sammut, P.; Willans, J. (Hrsg.): Proceedings of the First International Workshop Metamodeling for MDA. York, UK, November 2003, p. 178-197. http://www.omg.org/docs/ad/03-08-02.pdf (visited October 15, 2007)

[LDGR04]   Lawley, M.; Duddy, K.; Gerber, A.; Raymond, K.: *Language Features for Re-Use and Maintainability of MDA Transformations*. http://www.softmetaware.com/oopsla2004/duddy.pdf (visited November 25, 2007)

[OMG03]   Object Management Group: *MDA Guide Version 1.0.1.* June 1st, 2003. http://www.omg.org/docs/omg/03-06-01.pdf (visited November 4, 2008)

[QVT07]   Object Management Group: *Meta Object Facility (MOF) 2.0
             Query/View/Transformation Specification. Final Adopted Specification.*
             July 7, 2007. http://www.omg.org/docs/ptc/07-07-07.pdf
             (visited October 3, 2007)
[QVT08]   Object Management Group: *Meta Object Facility (MOF) 2.0
             Query/View/Transformation Specification Version 1.0* April 4, 2008
             http://www.omg.org/spec/QVT/1.0/PDF (visited November 4, 2008)

Modelling Graphical User Interfaces for embedded Systems

Georg Dummer, Thomas Schuster, Dennis Ritter, Klaus D. Müller-Glaser

FZI Forschungszentrum Informatik

Haid-und-Neu-Str. 10-14

76131 Karlsruhe

Germany

{dummer | schuster | ritter | kmg}@fzi.de

Abstract

In model-driven software development (MDSD) modelling of software artefacts is used for specification of software systems as a whole. Also in contrast to former case tool approaches, transformations are a central concept in order to move the models on to usable source code components. Although tool support on MDSD is growing it is not widely adopted today. One reason is that besides abundance of transformation engines is a lack of appropriate modelling languages for specialized application domains. Since the latter is triggered by missing metamodels we will present a metamodel that supports modelling of user interfaces for embedded systems. This metamodel is described by an UML profile. Furthermore we will demonstrate transformation rules to enact our modelling notation by a concrete use case scenario and thereby demonstrate the benefit of this approach.

1 Introduction

The design of embedded electronic systems in small and medium-sized enterprises (SME) changes nowadays towards accepted paradigms of software and system engineering. This is accompanied by a rapidly increasing complexity of embedded systems, which is a result of the today's requirements given by the needs of customers and industry. Furthermore new approaches in product engineering are often hard to establish due to monetary reasons or simply manpower shortage. In addition to make it even worse product cycles are getting shorter and shorter today.

An answer to shortened product and release cycles might by model-driven software development (MDSD), which provides the possibility to produce well-designed code by deduction from models [1] MDSD itself is not a new software development process but a method that may be integrated into any common process model [2]. By the means of MDSD software systems are specified through models on an abstract level. Throughout the phases of a chosen software development process, these models are transformed stepwise to more specialized models with a lower level of abstraction by model-to-model transformations. Finally these models are enacted by a model-to-text transformation, which transforms them to source code of the desired platform [3].

At present a bunch of different concrete types of MDSD can be observed, one of them, the Model Driven Architecture (MDA) published by the Object Management Group (OMG) [4]. So far the applicability of these approaches, including MDA, is still part of ongoing research. MDA is usually driven by models provided in Unified Modeling Language [5], [6]. Currently there are 13 types of diagrams specified by UML, also in order to focus specialized application domains UML provides the possibility to extend these diagrams by so called profiles. According to MDA models formulated by UML – or another Meta Object Facility (MOF)-compliant modelling language – depict a linchpin within the software development process if MDA is applied. Also communication and documentation is based on these models [8], [9]. Throughout the development the initial models are transformed to further models with more fine grained levels of abstraction, finally reflecting details of the target platform [1]. With the level of abstraction the roles of involved people change as well; for instance use cases might be suitable for a business or systems analyst, while a more detailed class diagram is presumably used by a system developer [8].

Considering development for a certain target domain, there are many details that cannot be covered by plain UML models [8], [10], this is one reason why CASE toolsets of the late nineties failed in practice [11]. Since MDSD suggests automatic transformation of models it is necessary to employ languages that are capable to represent objects of the target domain. In case of graphical user interfaces extensions to UML are therefore necessary (cf. section 2).

In this paper we will present an attempt to cover accurate specification of GUIs for embedded systems, through employment of UML-models. For demonstration purposes we will show how these models can be transformed through a primarily automated multistage process to the source code of a specific GUI-platform excerpted from real-world production code. In addition there is one transformation that manually enriches the model with some design information. We therefore introduce two lightweight extensions in terms of two UML profiles. Furthermore we make use of the openArchitecture-Ware framework (oAW) [12] to define rules for model-to-model and model-to-text transformations.

As shown in section 3 we concentrate our approach on the flexibility, general applicability and portability also taking different roles involved in a software development process with particular constraints of SMEs into account. These constraints concern qualitative and quantitative aspects. The core competence of a typical SME targeted in this paper lays on manufacturing systems engineering (MSE) which goes along with limited resources spent for software development. This underestimated significance of a flexible and efficient software development process is a challenge these SMEs have to meet.

The remainder of this paper is organized as follows: in section 2 we will introduce the state of the art in the context of MDA and especially modeling of user interaction and user interfaces. In section 3 we will present our extensions to UML and prepare a use case demonstration in section 4. As closure we will provide a summary and an outlook

30

on future work in this area.

2 State of the art

Since model-driven development has not yet reached the peak of inflated expectations it is still topic to ongoing research work [3], [7], [4]. While a rising demand for the construction of flexible and well-structured user interfaces [13], [14] creates a market for new development methods there are only few approaches to MDSD based construction of user interfaces. A first and straight approach to build a GUI is the use of 3rd party tools like easyGUI [15] or Embedded Wizard [16]. These kinds of tools are easy to handle (there is a well designed integration in existing tool chains), support a broad range of architectures and generate efficient code. Nevertheless this approach typically does not match the requirements of the MDA. A second way to create those user interfaces may be achieved by usage of declarative languages. Recent projects like XML User Interface Language (XUL) [17], eXtensible Application Markup Language (XAML) [18] or Views [19] take an XML-based approach for GUI description.

Considering typical software development processes an approach that involves several steps in order to construct software systems is reasonable [20], [21]. Since MDSD focuses on models as a central part of software development recent approaches have taken a course of action involving several levels of abstraction [22, cameleon Ref model, 1]. According to MDA the suggested modelling language is UML. Even exclusive of MDA, seeing that UML is a widely spread modelling language for system description, especially in object oriented design, several approaches employ UML for description of user interfaces. One of them is Pinheiro da Silva et al. who extend in [23], [24] the UML metamodel with new notational symbols or even new diagram types for specialized domains. Specification of user interfaces by the means of UML is described by Pinheiro da Silva et al. in "UML for interactive applications" (UMLi) in [24]. Almendros-Jimenez and Iribarne explore in [25], [26] the possibilities of native UML use case and activity diagrams. They use an extension to action elements in order to be able to parts typical for Java applets, therefore these models may only be used to generate GUIs working within Java applet. Without deep integration of a certain target language Lorenz [27] proposes a modelling technique for GUIs based on UML activity diagrams. He uses semi-formal UML annotations named "scenes" that specify details of a GUI. Furthermore he introduces, similar to Petrasch [7], two different types of actions, called user respectively system action to model user and system behaviour likewise. Based on the latter Schuster [28] and Link [22] created an extended UML metamodel, based on profiles, by which those "scenes" are replaced by a formal modelling method using UML Pins, thereby allowing a continuous MDSD approach.

While some approaches integrate details of their target platform on a modelling level and thereby circumvent seamless model transformation to other platforms, others propose more abstract notations to cover a more general approach. Yet only few of them consider the diversity of today's platforms. In a nutshell there is still a need for generalized and straightforward approaches to model-driven development of GUIs that allow toolsupported development of GUIs for any kind of target platform. The enacted modelling language should also be easy understandable and capable of being integrated to cur-

31

rent software development processes. Taking [27], [7], [28] and [22] into account, a generalization and further adaptation of these approaches promises to be successful in leveraging the current level of software development to higher stages in automation.

In the next section we present our approach of model-driven development of GUIs based on the discussed state of the art. We will thereby extend [28], [22]. By means of formal modelling we target at a general approach for any thinkable target platform in embedded systems engineering. Also this approach is flexible enough to apply it to common software development processes.

3 Model-driven Development of graphical user Interfaces

For the purpose of an enhanced conveyance of requirements – in the field of user interaction – from specification into concrete software systems the following approach will demonstrate a possibility to model user interactions on high level of abstraction and also provide transformation rules accompanied by lower level models in order to guide a development process down to source code of a desired platform. With the advent of model-driven software development graphical models are amplified by transformation processes that can step down to source code. As mentioned in section 2 a formal modelling technique that masks the needs of a specialized application domain is needed; in our case this domain is development of user interfaces in embedded system environments.

For an optimized support of different development processes and in order to cover our application domain we will first introduce a mechanism to cover GUI aspects in process models like UML activity diagrams, similar to [22], [27]. We will later consider activity diagrams as linchpin for a GUI development process. To provide a possibility for GUI enhancement we will present a GUI metamodel that is template for GUI refinements. This metamodel will cover common GUI elements without focusing on a certain platform. In order to conform to MDA we will also show transformation rules – model-to-model-transformation – that transform from activity diagrams to GUI models conform to the GUI metamodel. Finally we also provide a model-to-text transformation resulting in source code for a given menu engine.

3.1 Process Model Extension for Graphical User Interfaces

As mentioned above activity diagrams serve as the starting point of our approach to model use cases as refined by UML. These diagrams may represent platform independent models (PIM) in terms of MDA. According to this approach we had to move from a computation independent model (CIM) to a PIM [29]. Because standard activity diagrams are not meaningful enough to cover all needed GUI-related aspects they have to be extended by specialized model elements. Following [27] (cf. section 2), we introduce two new types of actions, which distinguish between System- and UserActions. This differentiation determines in a formal way if an action expects a user interaction, e.g. entering data or selecting a list element, or if the system itself is required to be active. We decide to make use of a UML profile to store our extensions in. This lightweight standard-extension mechanism of UML [5] remains fully compliant with the

UML 2.0 metamodel and therefore promises to be applicable in existing modelling projects based on UML.

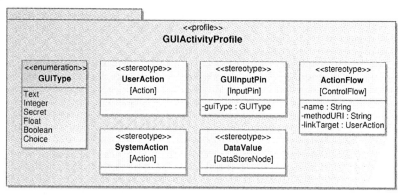

Figure 1. GUIActivityProfile

To specify a user action more in detail, we introduce another stereotype named GUIIn-putPin. As a specialization of a regular UML input pin, a GUIInputPin allocates an additional tagged value GUIType. A tagged value is a key-value pair which attaches supplementary information to a model element [4]. In this case every instance of the GUIInputPin has to have a GUIType. All available GUITypes themselves are given by an enumeration also included in the UML profile. Through this enumeration modelling is restricted to known elements reasonable for usage in a GUI, secondly the application of transformation rules is guaranteed. With GUIInputPins all attributes that need to be provided by the user and the type of these attributes can be modelled by choosing the corresponding GUIType. To ensure that e.g a GUIInputPin may not be applied to a SystemAction, an accordant constraint check exists in oAW's Check language. Figure 1 shows a partial view on our UML profile named GUIActivity-Profile. Using this profile adds GUI-relevant information to an activity diagram in a formal manner allowing for a tool-supported transformation.

While GUITypes describe what is needed, they do not comprise an assertion about concrete GUI elements. If e.g. a GUIInputPin is of GUIType Text, the corresponding GUI element could be an input field or a text area. So GUITypes are given as a declarative description for displayable elements. The advantage of this declarative description is twofold. First the GUIType does not make any restrictions on special GUI elements allowing for a variety of different GUI libraries. The precise mapping of GUI-Type to a GUI element is specified through transformation rules which we will describe later. A second advantage is found in the modelling itself. If a GUIType is not a simple type as Text or Boolean but complex, the refinement of this data type can be moved to the next phase in the software development process using e.g. XML Schema [30] as GUIType. This avoids mixing up different architect roles which would lead to disman-

33

tle the separation of concerns principle, which is especially not desirable for larger projects [8].

Having provided the extended activity diagrams, the next phase in the software development process can be addressed by a transformation to another PIM, the GUI model as presented in the next subsection.

3.2 A Metamodel for GUIs

GUIs in Embedded Systems are composed of a number of dialogue frames that are linked to each other in a specific way [14]. Moreover, these dialogues contain static and dynamic parts. All displayable elements form the static part of a GUI. The link structure and the way this structure is built can be regarded as the dynamic part of a GUI. Dynamic aspects can be described in additional navigational models [31] which we do not discuss further in this paper.

The above mentioned structure of a GUI with its linked dialogue modules requires the possibility to model the build-up of a single dialogue module and the complete GUI itself. We therefore introduce a second UML profile named GUIProfile based on a UML class diagram which supports the modelling of GUI-related development decisions. It can be used to model GUIs in a more detailed and formal way compared to standard UML. To assure independence of any GUI toolkits or libraries, the GUIProfile can be considered as a crosscut of many of the most common elements contained in currently available libraries like [27]. As mentioned in [12], the GUIProfile is easily extendable to meet future requirements for example by adding new elements to the corresponding enumeration.

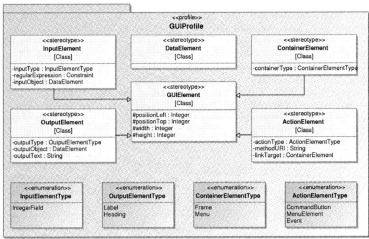

Figure 2. A Metamodel for modelling a GUI

If an UML activity diagram was extended with our `GUIActivityProfile` (cf. subsection 3.1) the first model-to-model (M2M) transformation can be applied to the GUI-model as an instance of `GUIProfile`. Each `GUIInputPin` of a `UserAction` is transformed to an instance of one stereotype of the `GUIProfile`. For example a `GUI-InputPin` of `GUIType` Text is transformed to an `InputElement` of `InputType` `TextField` or `TextArea` whereas a `GUIInputPin` of `GUIType` Boolean would be transformed to a `ChoiceElement` and so on. An example of a transformation rules that do a mapping between `GUIActivityProfile` and `GUIProfile` is shown in Figure 3. In our toolchain the oAW language `Xtend` is used to describe M2M transformations. The shown snippet describes partially how a `UserAction` is transformed into a dialog module. The first extension creates a package and a `ContainerElement` which represent the dialog module. Afterwards two different steps are performed. The first one creates everything that not depends on other `UserActions`. In the second step everything else is created. The second extension shows code that applies stereotypes and set tagged values.

```
uml::Package userAction2Package(uml::CallBehaviorAction
action,   uml::Model
model) :
    let c = model.addPackageAndContainerElement(action) :
    switch {
      case firstStep() : {
          c.addHeader() ->
          action.ownedElement.typeSelect(uml::InputPin).
          select(e|e.isGUIInputPin()).addInputElement(c)
          }
      case secondStep():
          getOutgoingFlows(action).

typeSelect(GUIActivityProfile::ActionFlow).addActionElement(
c)
      default: null
    } ->
    c.package;

private Void addHeader(uml::Class container) :
    let h=new Class:
    container.package.ownedType.add(h) ->
    h.applyStereotype("GUIProfile::OutputElement") ->
    h.setName("Header") ->

h.setValue(h.getAppliedStereotype("GUIProfile::OutputElement
"),
                "outputText", container.name) ->

h.setValue(h.getAppliedStereotype("GUIProfile::OutputElement
"),
            "outputType", OutputElementType::Header) ->
```

Figure 3. Transformation in Xtend

The first M2M transformation results in one GUI GUIProfile-model for each UserAction. In the next step during the design phase the GUI model can be manually enriched with further information that is not available by the extended activity diagram. For example the correct order of each GUI element, their sizes, colours etc. have to be specified as this information is of no concern during the preceding analysis phase. After the refinement of the GUI model, a second M2M transformation is applied. It transfers the GUI model to a platform specific model (PSM). The last model-to-text or model-to-code transformation (M2C) creates the finale source code like HTML or C++ source code. Similar to the M2M transformations the M2C transformation is written in oAW's Xpand language. The whole transformation process will be exemplified in section 4.

In conclusion our approach covers the major steps in a MDA process. Starting from an

extended UML activity diagrams, our GUI models which are instances of the GUIProfile are derived automatically from these extended activity diagrams. In the next step
the GUI model is manually enriched, transformed to a platform specific GUI model and
finally to specific platform code. Following the MDA approach, separating between
platform independent and a platform specific GUI model is essential in order to keep
device and platform independent as long as possible. Therefore we obtain reusable
transformations [4] and are able to increase the degree of automation in a software development process. Changing the GUI's target platform only requires replacing the last
M2C transformation rule with the appropriate one instead of writing the source code
again from scratch.

4 Practical Experience

To prove its suitability we present a realisation of our approach in this section based on a real-world. As a toolkit
for our work we chose the latest versions of MagicDraw
[32] and openArchitectureWare (oAW). We started by
creating the GUIActivityProfile and the GUI-
Profile (cf. section 3) as UML-profiles with Magic-
Draw. These profiles, of course, can be reused by other

MagicDraw projects or even other UML-tools. After this we implemented all necessary
Xtend and Xpand expressions in oAW.

4.1 Use Case

Designing a real world human-machine interface (HMI) of an embedded system will
serve as our case study. The design pattern of these interfaces is usually very similar, independent of the used display (text or dot matrix LCD) or buttons (discrete or soft
keys): after booting the system comes up with a main display layer. Pressing the EN-
TER button directs the user to the main menu. The main menu consists of a list of options which is navigatable by the UP and DOWN keys and selectable with ENTER leading to the next lower level. The ESC-button always allows the user to leave the current
level unchanged and enter the next higher level. This tree-structure ends up either in an
option list again or a screen for user interaction/information.

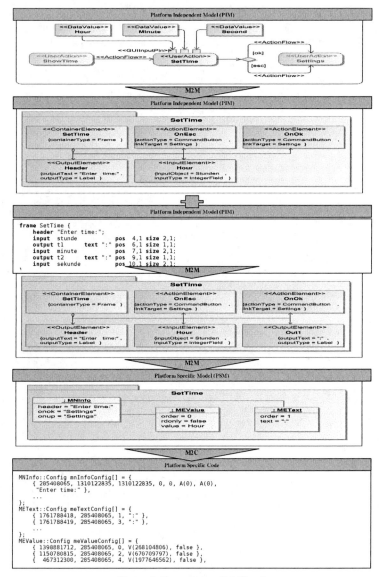

Figure 4: Case study „Set Time"

4.2 Specifying Use Cases with Activity Diagrams

In this step of the development process we start with use cases and choose one named "Set System Time" for further considerations. A system analyst specifies this use case by providing an activity diagram consisting of several User- and SystemActions with the help of the GUIActivityProfile. During the UserAction "System Time" (cf. figure 4) the user enters the new time, split in hours, minutes and seconds. The GUI has to provide the corresponding GUI elements so the system analyst simply adds GUIInputPins to the UserAction and assigns them with an adequate GUI-Type. The current implementation implicitly assigns an integer type because the presented HMI only uses numerical user inputs.

4.3 Activity Diagram to GUI Model Transformation

The aimed separation of roles requires that the system analyst only provide information about the attributes the user enters and doesn't care about the design or the layout of the corresponding GUI elements. This task is done by the GUI expert during a design phase. For this purpose the activity diagram is transformed by a M2M transformation to the corresponding PIM GUI model. The GUI expert enriches this model by adding information e.g. about the size of the input field Hour (c.f. figure 4) or the order of the different input elements. At this stage our GUI model is still independent of any platform or technology. Starting from the same refined and platform-independent GUI model, it is now possible to apply different M2M transformation rules to obtain platform-specific models for any desired platform. Finally the platform-specific model is transformed to source code by a M2C transformation. Figure 4 shows the whole approach exemplified for C++ configuration code for an existing interpreter (menu machine) as the target platform. To achieve the same GUI in linked HTML-pages for a fast preview we use the platform-independent GUI model, implement the transformation rules and again execute the transformation process. Finally we created two GUIs for two different platforms derived from one extended activity diagram. Although the initial effort to implement the needed UML profiles and the sets of transformation rules is not negligible the benefit of the initial complexity quickly pays off while reusing the set of transformation rules.

5 Conclusion

This paper demonstrates that the approach of model-driven software development is feasible and applicable for the development of graphical user interfaces of Embedded Systems even under probably limited conditions of a common SME. In order to permit a smooth integration in existing modelling techniques and frameworks the UML profile mechanism is used to provide GUI-related aspects. A multi-level MDA approach that accompanies the models transforms these aspects stepwise down to source code according to a common software development process. A real-world example serves as a case study demonstrating that transformations to several target platforms are possible. The benefit of this work is a seamless implementation of the MDA approach for modelling a graphical user interfaces: the model of GUIs does not only serve for communication or documentation purpose during the software development process but also as a real specification for artefacts created by transformation. It is used to generate source code and therewith becomes part of the implementation. The usage of different abstraction levels with corresponding models as required by the MDA has (beside the obvious disadvantages of increasing complexity and overhead) two major advantages: it makes our approach applicable to any common software development process and gives consideration to the diversity of platforms and devices used today. Additionally it can help to guarantee systems that really implement all modelled aspects and requirements. Whether the GUI has to be developed HTML based for a client/server architecture or for an Embedded System written in pure C, both GUIs can be derived using the same approach. In this first step we only address the modelling of one GUI per user interaction. Since the designs of graphical user interfaces of Embedded Systems tend to become more complex over the years other aspects like multiple users and different roles should be investigated and inserted into this approach in future research work.

References

[1]   G. Cernosek and E. Naiburg, "The Value of Modeling," IBM developerWorks, June 2004. http://www-128.ibm.com/developerworks/rational/library/6007.html

[2]   I. Sommerville, „Software processes" in Software Engineering, 7th ed. Harlow, UK: Pearson Education, 2004, pt. 1, ch. 4.

[3]   A. Kleppe, J. Warmer and W. Bast, MDA Explained: The Model DrivenArchitecture: Practice and Promise, Amsterdam, Netherlands: Addison-Wesley Longman, 2003.

[4]   J. Mukerji and J. Miller, "MDA Guide Version 1.0.1," OMG, 2003. http://www.omg.org/cgi-bin/doc?omg/03-06-01.

[5]   Unified Modeling Language (UML), Version 2.1.1: Superstructure, OMG Standard, 2007. http://www.omg.org/cgi-bin/doc?formal/07-02-03

[6]   J. Rumbaugh, I. Jacobson and G. Booch, "The Unified Modeling Language Reference Manual," 2nd Ed., Addison-Wesley, 2004.

[7]   R. Petrasch and O. Meimberg, Model Driven Architecture – Eine praxisorientierte Einführung in die MDA, Heidelberg, Germany: dpunkt, 2006.

[8]   P. Kruchten, The Rational Unified Process, An Introduction, 2nd ed., Addison-Wesley, 2000.

[9]   B. Hailpern and P. Tarr, "Model-driven development: The good, the bad, and the ugly," IBM Systems Journal, vol. 45, no. 3, 2006. http://www.research.ibm.com/journal/sj/453/hailpern.html

[10]   R. France and B. Rumpe, "Model-driven Development of Complex Software: A Research Roadmap," 2007 Future of Software Engineering, pp. 37–54.

[11]   Juhani Iivari: "Why are CASE tools not used?", Communications of the ACM archive, Volume 39 , Issue 10, October 1996, ISSN:0001-0782

[12]   http://www.openarchitectureware.org/

[13]   A. Arsanjani, "Service-oriented modeling and architecture," IBM developer-

Works, 2004. http://www.ibm.com/developerworks/library/ws-soa-design1/

[14] J. Bishop, "Multi-platform User Interface Construction – a Challenge for Software Engineering-in-the-Small," Proc. 28th Int. Conf. on Software engineering, Shang-hai, China, 2006.

[15] http://www.easygui.com/

[16] http://www.tara-systems.de/emwi/index.html

[17] XML User Interface Language (XUL) 1.0, Mozilla.org Specification. http://www.mozilla.org/projects/xul/

[18] Extensible Application Markup Language (XAML), Microsoft Specification. http://msdn2.microsoft.com/en-us/library/ms747122.aspx

[19] J. Bishop and N. Horspool, "Developing principles of GUI programming using views," SIGCSE Bulletin, ACM Press, 2004

[20] Philippe Kruchten: "The Rational Unified Process: An Introduction", Addison-Wesley Object Technology Series, Januar 2004, ISBN-10: 0321197704

[21] Michael W. Dietrich: „Das Microsoft Solutions Framework (Teil 1)", Juni 2004 http://msdn.microsoft.com/de-de/library/bb979125.aspx

[22] Stefan Link, Thomas Schuster, Philip Hoyer, Sebastian Abeck: "Focusing Graphi-cal User Interfaces in Model-Driven Software Development", IEEE Conference on Advances in Computer-Human Interaction (ACHI), Saint Luce, Martinique, Februar 2008

[23] P. Pinheiro da Silva, N. W. Paton, "User Interface Modelling with UML," Proc. 10th European-Japanese Conf. on Information Modelling and Knowledge Bases, Saariselk, Finnland, 2000.

[24] P. Pinheiro da Silva, N. W. Paton, "Improving UML Support for User Interface Design: A Metric Assessment of UMLi," Proc. 2003 Int. Conf. on Software Engi-neering.

[25] J. Almendros-Jimenez, L. Iribarne, "Describing use cases with activity charts," Proc. 2004 Metainformatics Symposium, pp. 141–159.

[26] J. Almendros-Jimenez, L. Iribarne, "Designing GUI components from UML Use Cases," Proc. 12th Int. Conf. and Workshop on the Engineering of Computer Based Systems, 2005, pp. 210–217.

[27] A. Lorenz, "Anpassung von UML-Aktivitäten an den Prozess der Webapplika-tionsentwicklung," Proc. 36. Jahrestagung der Gesellschaft für Informatik, Bre-men, Germany, 2006, pp. 178–184.

[28] Thomas Schuster: „Modellgetriebene Entwicklung grafischer Benutzer-schnittstellen: MDA im Einsatz", Vdm Verlag Dr. Müller, Dezember 2007, ISBN-10: 3836452596

[29] P. Forbrig, Objektorientierte Softwareentwicklung mit UML, Munich, Germany: Hanser Fachbuchverlag, 2006.

[30] XML Schema 1.0, W3C Recommendation, 2002. http://www.w3.org/XML/Schema

[31] N. Koch, "Transformation Techniques in the Model-Driven Development Process

41

of UWE," Proc. 6th Int. Conf. on Web Engineering, Palo Alto, USA, 2006.

[32] Nomagic: MagicDraw Website: http://www.magicdraw.com/

[All web references were valid as per Nov. 2008]

User Interfaces from Task Models

Peter Forbrig, Daniel Reichart, Andreas Wolff
University of Rostock
Chair of Software Engineering
Albert-Einstein-Str. 21
D-18051 Rostock
Germany
[peter.forbrig|daniel.reichart|andreas.wolff]@uni-rostock.de

Abstract

User-interface design is a very time consuming process. A lot of efforts have especially to be made if different platforms have to be supported. Different product lines have to be managed in this case. The paper presents a model-based development process based on task and dialog specifications. It especially focuses on a method of interactively developed platform specific user interfaces.

The notion of hierarchical dialog graphs is used to specify platform independent dialog models. Platform specific models are generated automatically. They are the basis for the generation of final user interfaces specified in XUL. While model-to-model transformations are used to construct a barebone and rough sketch of the UI, it is further refined and designed by using a well-integrated graphical editor. Limitations and expected boundaries of this approach are discussed as well.

1 Introduction

Model-based software development is becoming more and more popular because of its advantages in managing different versions of software for different platforms that are sometimes called product lines. Nowadays, the term model-based is often identified as part of the object-oriented development strategies related to UML only. However, the origins of using model specifications during software development come from task-based ideas. Originally such models were used to specify the behaviour of people. Later on task models became the basis for developing user interfaces.

For several years our group has been working on combining object-oriented and task-based methods. Our research is especially focused on using patterns for this purpose. However, this paper concentrates on a special problem of deriving different navigational models of different users and devices from general specifications. Nevertheless, it is necessary to introduce shortly the main ideas and models we are using within our development process.

Model-to-Model transformations based on Eclipse Foundations EMF [7], an implementation of W3C MOF meta-model, have been used in many fields of research and business. This paper illustrates another appliance. An EMF model describing possible navigation through a UI is used as transformation source model. Typical WIMP-style user-interfaces may, reasonably well, be described in this manner. In this paper openArchitectureWare (oAW) [17] workflow templates are used to transform dialog graphs into abstract user interface models (AUIs). Such AUI is a platform independent user-interface model.

For platform-specific user interfaces another type of model is used. UIs can be described, defined or programmed in many different ways. Closely related to model-based development are any types of XML-based UI-languages. Their main advantage is an available well-defined grammar and their hierarchical structure.

While several XML-based UI languages are wide-spread; XAML (Microsoft .NET), UsiXML and XUL (Mozilla) certainly are of major importance. Transformations of this paper produce XUL-models as target model.

The paper is structured in the following way. After this short introduction chapter 2 presents our notations of task models and dialog graphs. Afterwards it is shown how tools can be used to support the development from task models to dialog graphs. Afterwards, strategies for automatically generated platform specific navigation dialogs and possibilities to modularize dialogs are discussed. The transformation from dialog graphs to user interfaces is discussed in chapter 3. Chapter 4 relates our ideas to existing publications and finally in chapter 4 some closing remarks are presented.

2 Model-based Software development

2.1 Task Models

Our software development methodology is based models of psychologists and on man-power studies. According to these studies, a task has to be performed on an artefact by a person in a certain role using tools. Additionally, some tasks have to be executed on devices with certain features only. In an abstract way a task can be considered as specification of the following form:

Task = (Goal, Sub-tasks, Temporal Relations, Pre-conditions, Post-conditions
   Artefact, Tool(s), Role(s), Device)

The notation of concurrent task trees (CTT) has nearly become a standard in representing tree structures of tasks.

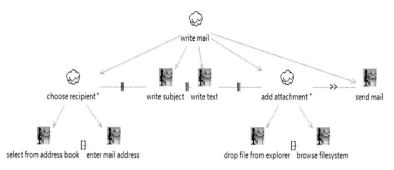

Fig. 1. Task model for ordering different kinds of dishes (taken from [29])

Fig. 1 gives an impression of the notation of temporal relations of task models. Writing a mail can be done in different ways. The temporal relation ||| means order independence. The selection of the recipient can be done in two different ways according to the temporal relation choice ([]). The temporal relation ">>" (enabling) specifies that the execution of the first task enables the second one to be executed. Details of the tasks like the roles that are responsible for executing it are hidden here for reasons of readability.

2.2 Dialog Models

Due to our development strategy, we specify the navigation structure of an interactive system by a special graph, which is called dialog graph.

A dialog graph consists of a set of nodes, which are called views and a set of transitions. There are 5 types of views: single, multiple, modal, complex and end views. A single view is an abstraction of a single sub-dialog of the user interface that has to be described. A multiple view serves to specify a set of instances of a sub-dialog. A modal view specifies a sub-dialog, which has to be finished in order to continue other sub-dialogs of the system. Complex views allow hierarchical descriptions of a user interface model. Nodes can be specified in this way by graphs. End views are final points of (sub-)dialogs. Each view is characterized by a set of navigational and interaction elements.

A transition is a directed relation between an element of a view and another view or element. Transitions reflect navigational aspects of user interfaces. It is distinguished between sequential and concurrent transitions. A sequential transition from view v1 to view v2 closes the sub-dialog described by v1 and activates the sub-dialog, which corresponds to v2. In contrast, v1 remains open while v2 is activated if v1 and v2 are connected by a concurrent transition. Fig. 2 presents the graphical notation for the different types of views and transitions.

Fig. 2. Symbols for possible transitions and views within a dialog-graph

There are some constrains between view type and transition type. Multiple views e.g. should have incoming transitions of type concurrent. Such transitions allow generating several instances of the same dialog by executing them several times. A dialog graph with multiple views must have concurrent transitions. Otherwise it is impossible to get several instances.

To get an impression how dialog graph look like, a dialog graph for the task of using a mail client was developed. Fig. 3 demonstrates the example of our mailing system with single views (main window, write mail), multiple views (read mail) and the end view (end).

The graph was produced using our eclipse [8] plug-in DiaTask. This tool was developed at our department in a model-based (UML) way using the Eclipse Modeling Framework (EMF) [7].

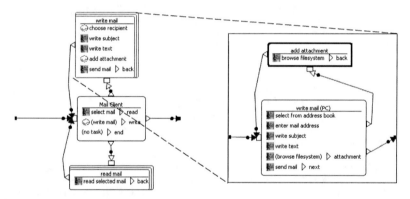

Fig. 3. Dialog graph for using a mail client

DiaTask allows assigning several different dialog graphs to one task model, which give freedom for a lot of experiments. Additionally, this feature allows specifying the co-operation of different roles using different specification of dialog graphs.

Next section will especially focus on tool support for the development step from task models to dialog specifications.

2.3. From task models to dialog graphs

Currently we are working on two strategies for developing dialog models. On the one hand, we allow designers to specify hierarchical dialog specifications, which are the basis for the generation of dialog graphs for different platforms. On the other hand, we provide automatic transformations from task models to different platform specifications.

2.3.1 Hierarchical dialog specification

Using this approach, a designer has to decide, how many views are desired, and whether each of them is modal, single, multiple or complex. Afterwards he has to assign relevant tasks to views. The underlying task model determines the set of available tasks. Furthermore, the designer has to model transitions between views that are related to tasks. **Fig. 4** gives an impression of how the tool that supports this development step looks like.

At the right hand side of one can see a task tree. The editor for dialog graphs is located in the centre. Transitions can be attached to a task. A task can be selected by simply clicking on it. The editor visualizes which task is attached to a certain transition.

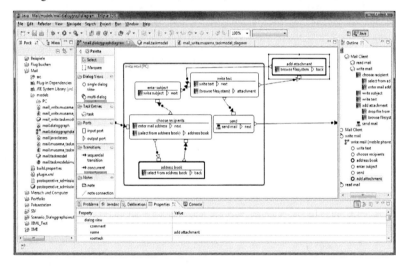

Fig. 4. Screenshot of the dialog-graph editor

Using our tool two types of behavioural specifications are combined; task models and dialog specifications. This information can be used for animations like those described in []. In this paper we focus on dialog graphs for different platforms.

Fig. 5 gives an impression of the differences in resulting graphs for two different platforms. Starting point is the navigation dialog specification of **Fig. 3**. It has to be constrained to the platform of a mobile. Certain tasks like "drop file from explorer" or "browse file system" are not available for that device. That is the reason why the right-hand part of the specification of **Fig. 3** has to be replaces like sketched in **Fig. 5**.

There has to be specified a specific dialog graph for every target platform and role combination. This seems to be achievable in our example. In general there could be *n* user roles and *m* platform within one application. Thus it results in n * m different dialog graphs. Those would have to be developed and maintained later on. Even in the case of n=3 and m=3 this is not a trivial task.

The question arises whether this process could be automated in such a way that the platform specific specifications are generated in an automatic way. Originally it was our idea to specify dialog graphs for different devices and afterwards generate variations for each role. Experiences in projects with partners from industry resulted in an approach that is based on designing navigation models for roles and derive the variations for different devices.

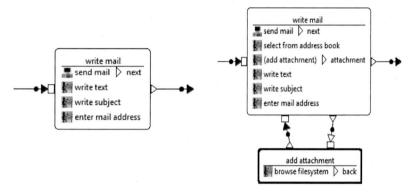

Fig. 5. Part of the navigation dialog of task model from Fig. 1 for two different platforms

Our concept of complex views allows us to hierarchically group different graphs on different levels. This gives the opportunity to group views according to screen size of devices. Let us assume that we have device types like mobile, PDA and PC. **Fig. 6** demonstrates an abstract general hierarchical dialog graph for a role that has to be supported by these three different devices. Additionally, **Fig. 6** presents the corresponding three dialog graphs, which can be extracted from the general model.

However, the sketched transformation is not sufficient. Some further actions have to be performed. Tasks might have to be removed from certain views if they are not supported by the specific device. A problem occurs if all task of one view vanish. Consequently, the whole view has to be deleted. This happened in our mail example with the view for attaching a file. However, in this example there was no problem with preceding and succeeding views. Due to this fact deleting of the view was no problem. In fact, it can happen that there exists a sequence of transitions and by deleting one view further connections of the preceding view are missed.

In this case the preceding view has to be connected with succeeding views of the deleted dialog. This is possible without problems if both mentioned transitions have the same type. More ore less two transitions are unified to one transition by omitting the dialog in between.

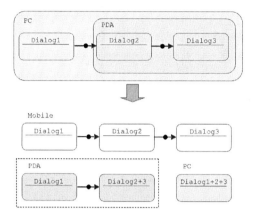

Fig. 6. Derivation of platform specific dialog graphs

If there are different types of transition the resulting type can be derived from incoming and outgoing transition. If one of both is concurrent the resulting type is concurrent as well.

2.3.2 Transformation from tasks to dialogs

As an alternative to hierarchical dialog specifications we consider direct transformations from task models to platform specific dialog graphs. The concept and the corresponding tool support are discussed in Diebow [4].

His concept is based on the idea of extending nodes of operator-centric task trees by information that specifies whether nodes are grouped into one view or distributed into different views. **Fig. 7** presents task model of **Fig. 1** in an operator-centric way.

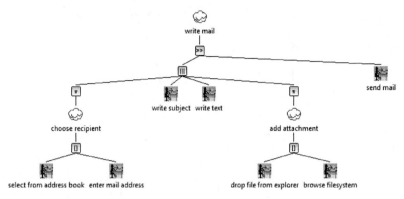

Fig. 7. Task model in an operator-centric notation

Designers can manually attach the additional information into the editor or they can specify a general profiles for operators that are used during the transformation process. One can add the following types of flags:

ICV - Integrate Children into View: Node and direct children are atttached to one single view

IN   - Ignore Node -Node and direct and indirect children ar ignored

PUNM   - Pick Up for Navigation Model – Abstract tasks are included into the navigaton model

VL   - View List – Explicite grouping and ordering of children

Fig. 8 gives an example of attachd flags and their consequences.

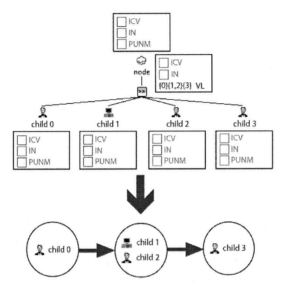

Fig. 8. Task tree attached with flags and the resulting dialog graph.

In **Fig. 8** the abstract task is ignored and the children are grouped according to the explicite ordering specification. Activating ICV imstead of the explicite grouping would result in one view only.

Such profiles can be specified platform dependant. Manual attached information is stored platform specific as well.

It is also possible to combine both strategies. Manually attached information rewrites the specification from profiles.

3 Transformation from dialog graphs to XUL

This chapter describes how dialog-graph models are converted into user interface prototypes of applications.

3.1 Dialog Graph Meta Model

As mentioned above, our transformations do make use of openArchitectureWare workflows. They transform an EMF model of a dialog graph into an abstract user interface model which is defined using XUL.

51

Fig. 8 shows the meta-model of dialog graphs. Stereotypes *Model* and *ModelElement* refer to their respective EMF meta-model types, as well as *EBoolean* is EMF's Boolean type. Classes *Task*, *DeviceType* and *UserRole* are defined in other packages; those are non-displayed as their actual declaration is of no importance for this paper.

Any view of a dialog graph is modeled as *DialogView*. Views have references to their respective tasks and possibly to necessary artifacts. Inter-view navigation is controlled via ports. A port is either source or target of a transition

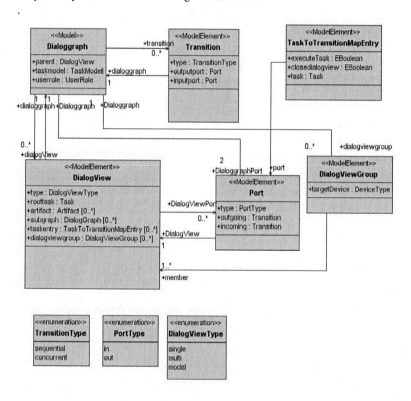

Fig. 9. Meta-model of dialog graph

The completion of a task may result in a transition. Such transitions are specified in class *TaskToTransitionMapEntry*. Each conditional transition referring to ports of a view is stored within its *DialogView.taskentry* attribute.

The meta-model provides means to define hierarchical dialog specifications which were introduced in paragraph 2.3.1. Class *DialogViewGroup* is used entirely for hierarchical dialog graphs. A parent-child relationship is established between instances of *Dialoggraph* and *DialogView*, navigatable as *parent* or rather *subgraph*.

3.2 Mapping Templates

As mentioned above we strive to generate an interface whose mock-up can be viewed, and thus discussed, in a common viewer. We decided on a combination of HTML and XUL for that purpose. A suitable viewer would be every Gecko-based web-browser; Firefox is probably the most well-known example.

To generate an UI, using meta-model of **Fig. 8**, as first step a starting point needs to be identified. Our basic WIMP-style application consists of view and simple interaction objects arranged in the view. Any application must have a start view configured in its dialog-graph.

Dialog-graph inter-view transitions are defined using a port-to-port metaphor. Application start- and end-nodes fit into this system as well. There is a port defined as application-start, type outgoing and named 'start', and there is an opposite a port, type incoming and named 'in', denoting end-of-application. Objects of type Dialoggraph contain references to those entry and exit ports within their attribute *DialoggraphPort*.

For generating our application's startup mask we begin transformations in the context of the root Dialoggraph. Here the application's entry port is identified by OCL and an oAW template is invoked by:

«EXPAND Dialoggraph (DialoggraphPort.selectFirst(port|port.type.toString()=='in'))»

This code is embedded into a HTML skeleton to provide a valid page. That skeleton source-code is omitted here.

Our templates translate each *DialogView* into a separate XUL file; each such file has a name derived from its view's name. Therefore a startup mask for our kind of application needs to provide a HTML-link to the respective XUL file that contains the transformed view. Navigating along the meta-model start-view can be identified as: «LET start-Port.outgoing.inputport.DialogView AS startView». Using *startView* it is simple to identify the XUL file to link to; HTML source code for that purpose would be something along: <a href="«startView.name».xul">Start Prototype</a>.

Transformation of each *DialogView* to XUL yields an interface description which we consider as abstract user interface. *Task*s are converted into buttons, taking their *name* as button label.

*Transition*s are always assigned to tasks; this is reflected on XUL level as well. Every transition is compiled into a JavaScript based navigation instruction, which gets annotated as attribute of above task buttons. Thus transitions are translated as:

onclick="window.open('«targetPort.DialogView.name».xul', [..]

Fig. 10 illustrates a view's transformation result. Source was the left view of fig. 5. Within this view a transition from task "send mail" also was specified. Its representation certainly is not visible in **Fig. 10**, but a click on button "send mail" would invoke the next window.

53

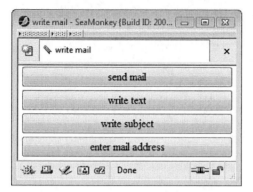

Fig. 10. Transformation result (abstract canoncical prototype), viewed in a web-browser

Along with view-transitions, tasks are attributed with a number of different information to eventually, in future, generate applications with task models. Besides generating a mere UI prototype in XUL, references to that information is also carried over into the resulting XUL. Thus, in the next steps we are able to post-process our generated user-interface in a specialized XUL editor [32], changing its layout and design, while keeping it as a working prototype.

A user interface designer has to proceed in the following way. At first he has to select a visualization (graphical element) of a task (e.g. a button), choose "replace", and select via "drag & drop" a graphical element or a predesigned component, which replaces the original one. To proceed in this way makes it possible to maintain taskrelated associations of an element and accordingly keep connections to the task model.

In this way edited user interfaces specified in XUL can be still included into the animation of the canonical prototype. They can be further refined to the final look and feel. **Fig. 11** gives an impression how this looks like within the eclipse environment.

The upper part of **Fig. 11** visualises the UI a user can interact with. In the lower part one can see the animated task model. This animated prototype is very helpful in partoicipative software development to check in a very early stage the requirements and the expectations of users.

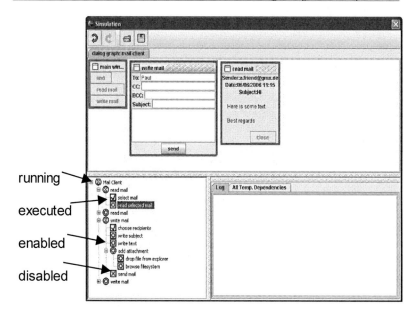

Fig. 11. Animated task model and animated user interface

4 Related Work

There have been developed a lot of methodologies and tools for model-based development of interactive systems. We want to concentrate on approaches that we consider as the most typically and most promising ones.

This is on the one side TERESA [27] within the Cameleon project [1]. On the other side, there exists UsiXML [29], a language, a set of models and a tool set. Both approaches do not have navigation specifications like dialog graphs. More or less this information is contained in different other models.

TERESA generates the user interface based on the models by presenting all tasks active at the same time in one window. Additionally some heuristics are used.

TERESA and UsiXML do not really have the abstraction level of a dialog graph. They have the idea of an abstract user interface (AUI), which is a little bit more concrete than our approach. Our dialog graphs are more concrete than task models but more abstract than AUIs.

Unlike to TERESA and UsiXML our dialog graph gives the opportunity for an explicit design process of the navigation structure. Our approaches can be offered as alternative strategies to software developers, if the generation process does not deliver the expected results. On the other hand one can save time if the automatic generation process delivers already acceptable results. It might depend on the application domain and especially on the number of tasks in the model, which approach fits best. Especially for larger task models our approach might fit better because not all tasks are presented that could be executed in a certain moment. Views contain only selected tasks of the enabled task set.

We are sure that our ideas can be integrated into the toolset of UsiXML. At the moment we have a look at the possibility to go this way and to use UsiXML for our tools. We also would like to extend UsiXML by the concepts of roles.

The approach proposed by Costa et. al. [2] uses a kind of task trees represented in UML notation for dialog modelling. Each task element is detailed by the Dialog Model using a UML-compliant adaptation of the CTT notation. Tool support is available by DialogSketch [15]. Canonical abstract prototypes are used to specify the first level of user interfaces. In this way it does not have this level of abstraction we want to support to. It is focused on Web interfaces and related papers do not discuss the problem of different roles and a variety of platforms.

We recognized that most publications related to navigation specifications are related to the area of Web applications. This was the result of a current survey of the literature.

Leung et. al. [12] specify navigation for web applications by state charts. They present specification solutions for intra-page, inter-page and frame-based navigation by hierarchical states. They already raise the problem of multiple windows that are specified in dialog graphs as multiple views. Their solution suggests separate state charts for each window. The authors identified dynamic content as a special problem of their kind of specification. From our point of view the readability is another problem. The notation is much more complex than our dialog graphs. It also does not allow different kinds of transitions. Roles and devices were not considered.

Koch [11] as well focuses her work on WEB modelling. She bases her specification on UML [30]. UWE (UML-based Web Engineering) is a model-driven development approach. Class diagrams with special profiles specify the navigation model. More or less only the menu structure is represented by the specification. It is the goal of this approach to transform navigation models together with business specifications in form of activity diagrams and state charts to service-oriented applications.

Very similar approaches are presented by Quinterio et.al. [22] and Ricci and Schwabe [25]. Class diagrams specify the navigation and the application domain are service-based applications as well.

Hierarchies of specifications are not considered in both cases.

5 Summary and Outlook

Within the paper we presented in a very short way our general idea of model-based development of interactive systems. There was a special focus on task models and dialog specifications.

The center of the paper was the idea to develop one task model and afterwards navigation dialogs for every role. In order to automatically generate dialog graphs for different platforms in a manual way a general all-embracing hierarchical specification is suggested. Low levels in the hierarchy correspond to low-level platforms and high levels in the hierarchy correspond to high-level platforms with a lot of features. Transformation rules are available that help to sidestep problems during the generation process of platform specific dialog graphs.

Furthermore a modularization concept for dialog graphs was introduced that is based on interface descriptions by pins. It is the intention of this approach to integrate already implemented components into the specification process and to allow using the implemented parts while animating the specification as an abstract canonical prototype [6].

Actually we are working on a usage of patterns. They shall help to transform existing models to more elaborated ones [23]. Reuse of knowledge should be possible in this way [10]. The development of models becomes much more economical by using predefined and evaluated patterns.

We also study the relation of patterns and components and how patterns can be implemented by components on different platforms. It seems to be possible to exchange components for patterns according to the actual context of use.

The concept of patterns may also help to maintain software and to support reengineering processes.

References

1. Cameleon: http://giove.cnuce.cnr.it/cameleon.html. (visited November 4, 2008)

2. Costa, D., Nóbrega, L., Nunes, N.: An MDA Approach for Generating Web Interfaces with UML ConcurTaskTrees and Canonical Abstract Prototypes, TAMODIA 2006, Hasselt, Belgium, October 23-24, 2006.

3. CTTE: The ConcurTaskTree Environment. http://giove.cnuce.cnr.it/ctte.html. (visited November 4, 2008)

4. Diebow, Ch.: Entwicklung eines Konzeptes zur interaktiven Trtansformation von Aufgabenmodellen in Navigationsmodelle, Master Thesis, University of Rostock, 2008.

5. Dittmar, A., Forbrig, P.: The Influence of Improved Task Models on Dialogues. *Proc. of CADUI 2004*, Madeira, 2004.

6. Dittmar, A., Forbrig, P., Reichart, D.: Model-based Development of Nomadic Applications. In *Proc. of 4th International Workshop on Mobile Computing,* Rostock, Germany, 2003.

7. EMF: http://www.eclipse.org/modeling/emf/?project=emf (visited November 4, 2008)

8. Eclipse: http://www.eclipse.org. (visited November 4, 2008)

9. Elwert, T., Schlungbaum, E.: Dialogue Graphs – A Formal and Visual Specification Technique for Dialogue Modelling. In Siddiqi, J.I., Roast, C.R. (ed.) *Formal Aspects of the Human Computer Interface*, Springer Verlag, 1996.

10. Javahery, H., Sinnig, D.,Seffah, A.,Forbrig, P., Radhakrishnan, T.: Pattern-Based UI Design: Adding Rigor with User and Context Variables, Tamodia 2006, Hasselts, Belgium, 2006.

11. Koch, N.: Transformation Techniques in the Model-Driven Development Process of UWE, ICWE'06 Workshop, Palo Alto, 2006

12. Leung, K.R.P.H., Hui, L.C.K., Yiu, S.M., Tang, R.W.M.: Modeling Web Navigation by Statechart, Proc. COMPSAC'00

13. Limbourg, Q., Vanderdonckt, J.: Addressing the Mapping Problem in User Interface Design with USIXML, *Proc TAMODIA 2004*, Prague, P. 155-164

14. López-Jaquero, V., Montero, F. , Molina, J.,P., González, P.: A Seamless Development Process of Adaptive User Interfaces Explicitly Based on Usability Properties, *Proc. EHCI-DSVIS'04*, p. 372-389, 2004.

15. Luyten, K., Clerckx, T., Coninx, K., Vanderdonckt, J.: Derivation of a dialog model from a task model by activity chain extraction. In Jorge, J., Nunes, N.J., e Cunha, J.F. (ed.), *Proc. of DSV-IS 2003*, LNCS 2844, Springer, 2003.

16. Nóbrega, L., Nunes, N. J. and Coelho, H.: DialogSketch: Dynamics of the Canonical Prototypes, TAMODIA'2005, Gdansk, Poland, September 26-27, 2005.

17. openArchitectureWare: http://www.openarchitectureware.org/ (visited November 4, 2008)

18. Paterno, F., Mancini, C., Meniconi, S: ConcurTaskTrees: A Diagrammatic Notation for Specifying Task Models, *Proc. Interact 97*, Sydney, Chapman & Hall, p362-369, 1997.

19. Paterno, F., Santoro, C.: One Model, Many Interfaces. In Proc. of the Fourth International Conference on Computer-Aided Design of User Interfaces, p. 143-154. Kluwer Academics Publishers, 2002.

20. Paquette, D., Schneider, K.: Interaction Templates for Constructing User Interfaces from Task Models, Proc. Of CADUI 2004, Madeira Island, Portugal, p. 221-232

21. Puerta, A.R. and Eisenstein, J.: Towards a General Computational Framework for Model-Based Interface Development Systems. Proc. of the 4th ACM Conf. On Intelligent User Interfaces IUI'99 (Los Angeles, 5-8 January 1999). ACM Press, New York (1999), 171–178

22. Quintero, R., Torres, V., Ruiz, M., Pelechanto, V,: A Conceptual Modeling Approach for the Design of Web Applications based on Services, Proc. ACM SE'06, Melbourne, USA, March, 2006

23. Radeke, F., Forbrig, P., Seffah, A., Sinnig; D.: PIM Tool: Support for Pattern-Driven and Model-Based UI Development, Tamodia 2006, Hasselts, Belgium, 2006

24. Reichart, D., Forbrig, P., Dittmar, A.: Task Models as Basis for Requirements Engineering and Software Execution, Proc. of. Tamodia 2004, p. 51-58

25. Ricci, L. A., Schwabe, D.: An Authoring Environment for Model-Driven Web Applications, Proc. WebMedia'06, Natal, Brazil, 2006

26. Sinnig, D., Gaffar, A., Reichart, D., Forbrig, P., Seffah, A.: Patterns in Model-Based Engineering, *Proc. of CADUI 2004*, Madeira, 2004.

27. Sinnig, D., Javahery, H., Forbrig, P. and Seffah, A., "Patterns and Components for Enhancing Reusability and Systematic UI Development", in Proceedings of HCI International, Las Vegas, USA, 2005.

28. Teuber, C., Forbrig, P.: Modeling Patterns for Task Models, Proc. of Tamodia 2004, Prague, Czech. Republic, p. 91-98.

29. TERESA: http://giove.cnuce.cnr.it/teresa.html (visited November 4, 2008)

30. UML: http://www.uml.org (visited November 4, 2008)

31. UsiXML: http://www.usixml.org/ (visited November 4, 2008)

32. Wolff, A., Forbrig, P., Dittmar, A., Reichart, D.: Linking GUI Elements to Tasks – Supporting an Evolutionary Design Process, Proc. of. Tamodia 2005, Gdansk, Poland, p. 27-34

33. XUL: http://www.xul.org (visited November 4, 2008)

HCI Patterns in the Context
of Model Driven Development™ for Interactive Systems

Roland Petrasch
TFH Berlin
Luxemburger Str. 10
13353 Berlin
Germany
roland.petrasch@tfh-berlin.de

Max Bureck
qme Software
Gustav-Meyer-Allee 25
13355 Berlin
Germany
max.bureck@qme-software.de

Abstract

Model driven software development approaches like OMG's *Model Driven Architecture*™ (MDA™) or *Model Driven Development*™ (MDD™), use separate models (computation independent models), platform independent models, platform model and platform specific models making the essential parts of a system reusable and independent from different technologies. Another advantage of this separation and the high degree of formalization in the early stages of a project are an improved maintainability and portability of the software system, because all or main parts of it are automatically generated from the models.

A formal (or semi-formal) modeling language like the UML can be used for the MDA and is in principle suitable for interactive systems, but there are no specific language constructs and diagrams for the modeling of user interfaces. On one side it is not clear how to use the UML in conjunction with software-ergonomic requirements in the context of the development of interactive systems. Patterns for the Human-Computer Interface (HCI) can contribute to narrow the gap between the UML and User Interface Design. On the other side HCI Patterns are available a fairly long time and can successfully be used for as a usability engineering technique

This article explains the fundamentals of HCI Patterns in conjunction with MDA. The concept for such *Model Based User Interfaces* (MBUI) is part of a joint research project.

Keywords: Model Based Software Development, Model Driven Development, MDD, MDA, Model Driven Development, Model Driven Architecture, UI Modeling, User Interface, Model Based User Interface, HCI, Human Computer Interaction, HCI Pattern, Usability, Software-Ergonomics.

1. Introduction

The relevance of software ergonomic aspects during the development of interactive systems is without controversy. According to a study in 1992, the effort for user interface design activities (including programing) is approximately 50% [Myer92] and today probably requires a similar amount due to the fact that requirements to interactive systems have increased. web 2.0 applications are a good example for this trend. Another reason for the high expenditure is degree of automation for GUI development that is relatively low compared to the persistence layer for instance: Code generation techniques based on abstract HCI concepts are not widespread in practice while PoJOs, entity classes and business logic can be easily generated from UML models.

Since 10 years HCI Patterns are known in the context of software engineering, e.g. [Cora96], [Tidw98]. They can be considered a „natural advancement" of design patterns. However, the definitions for the notion *pattern* are quite general and imprecise, e.g.: "Patterns are abstract, core solutions to problems that recur in different contexts but encounter the same 'forces' each time." [Grah03].

Not surprisingly many pattern languages are available [Bayl98], [Brad98], [Grah03], [Tidw99], [Welie03] and a discussion is going on, what requirements on patterns and pattern languages should be defined. Borchers for instance criticized the lack of understandability of GoF patterns [Gamm95] for non-professionals [Borc00][1].

Despite these open issues HCI patterns (and design patterns) are accepted by experts and to a limited extend used in practice. It makes sense to integrate HCI patterns into model driven development. For some time software manufacturers strive to produce software products like „industrial" goods, i. e. code is generated automatically on the basis of reusable models and other artifacts. Pattern can play an important role when it comes to (re)use commonly accepted solutions on the model and also code level.

The starting point for HCI patterns in the context of model based development is OMG's MDA (chapter 2). A brief introduction to model-based user interfaces and HCI patterns is given in chapter 3 before patterns in the MDA-context are explained in chapter 4.

---

1 He comes to the following conclusion: „The Gang of Four book contains no patterns"

2. Model Driven Architecture

OMG's *Model Driven Architecture* (MDA) describes the vision of interoperability, integration, variety and coexistence of software systems. *Computation* and *Platform Independent Models* (CIM / PIM) can be transformed to *Platform Specific Models* (PSM), so that the business data and logic can be separated from the underlying platform technology. This leads to a better re usability of (design) models and less effort for the maintenance because of the formal and consistent specification [MDA, S. 1-2]. Another main advantage is the code generation and the reduction of manually programmed code fragments [Petr06].

For modeling every textual or graphical language conform to the MOF standard (Meta Object Facility) can be used, e.g. the UML [UML]. Queries and views for models and model transformations are specified in MOF QVT (Query, Views, Transformations) standard [QVT].

Since the MDA does not provide a (standard) process, a individual model driven methodology is to be defined, e.g. for the number and types of transformations. However, the MDA guide describes the MDA pattern and diverse derivations by which a PIM is transformed to a PSM (s. fig. 1). Also viewpoints are defined: *Computation Independent Viewpoint, Platform Independent Viewpoint* and *Platform Specific Viewpoint* [MDA, S. 2–3].

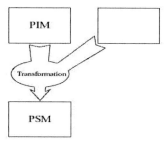

Fig. 1:MDA pattern for Transformation [MDA, S. 2–7]

OMG's MDA does not provide any information about special development aspects like the user interface design, because it is a general approach independent from a concrete software architecture or development method. In the following, a model driven and pattern based approach for the development of software systems with a user interface is presented.

3. User Interface Design and HCI Patterns

3.1 Development Process for interactive Systems

For the development of the HCI (Human Computer Interface) the ISO 13407 specifies a *Human-Centred Design Process for Interactive Systems* [ISO13407] that consists of 5 steps.

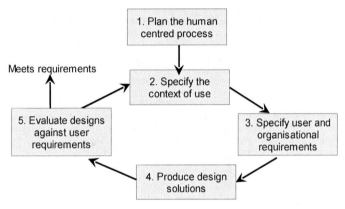

Fig. 2: Human Centred Design (UCD) Process (ISO 13407 [ISO13407])

The d*esign process* ends when the requirements are met (s. fig. 3). Based on this process a pattern oriented approach can be defined. A precondition for this are model based user interfaces that are explained in the next chapter.

3.2 Model-Based HCI-development

Modeling, according to the MDA, implies abstraction from the platform a system is created for, that is the HCI-models abstract from the basic UI-system (e.g. JSP, KDE, SWT, Swing). There have been various languages and forms of notation for such an abstract description for more than 20 years, e.g. multi-party-grammars, state-charts, petri-nets, and other, special forms of notation like *User Action Notation* [Hart90]. Some of them are not based on a meta-model, are not MOF-compliant respectively, so a use for the MDA would be (too) complex.

That is why approaches using UML-profiles or at least approaches similar to UML seem to be more promising. Languages using the UML-profile-mechanism (lightweight approach) are GUILayout [Blan04], Wisdom [Nune01], and UWE [Koch01], among others. More heavyweight technologies, such as UMLi [Silv02], [Silv03] work with their own meta-models. Below, we will consider UML-profiles, due to easy adaptability. Also, we won't analyse XML-based languages, such as UIML [Phan00] or webML [Ceri03] [2].

In practice, however, *User-Interface Builders* for particular platforms are still the prevalent technologies. The formal, meta-model based techniques mentioned above where only used in few cases. With the availability of powerful modeling- and MDA-tools, as well as corresponding standards, e.g. XMI for model-exchange, methods for a platform-independent UI-modeling in conjunction with generators will become more applicable.

The following extract from the MBUI (*Model Based User Interface*) project will help to clarify the subject. As an example for the UI-modeling basis the *MBUI-Profile*, providing a set of stereotypes, is used. The stereotypes used in the example are defined as extensions to the meta-classes Class and Association. For example there is a Dialog and an Area, where interaction-elements (I_Element) can be placed on.

Interaction-elements, such as as buttons (Button) and text-fields (TextField), are elements that can offer interactions (Interaction). A special case of an interaction is the navigation, which connects interaction-elements with each other. Figure 3 depicts an extract of the MBUI profile and provides an example of the extension-relationship to the meta-classes from the UML kernel-package [UML].

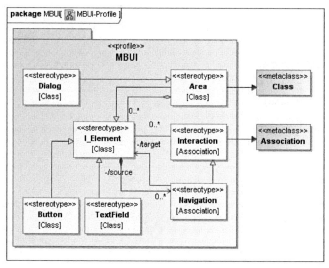

Fig. 3: MBUI-Profile (extract)

---

2   Please note that it is generally quite easy to transform XML-based approaches to UML-Profiles.

The level of abstraction was restricted intentionally: E.g. for reasons of understandability the stereotype «Button» implies a visual user interface. It is possible to define other abstractions with appropriate UML profiles.

A concrete UI-concept for an interactive application can now use these stereotypes. As an example an application for flight booking is chosen. It offers a booking-dialog (FlightBooking) that owns a button for booking (Book). Before the flight is booked bindingly, a feedback-dialog (BookingFeedback) asks the user to verify the booking (Yes) or decline it (No) (s. fig. 4). Only after positive feedback the confirmation (BookingConfirm) is shown.

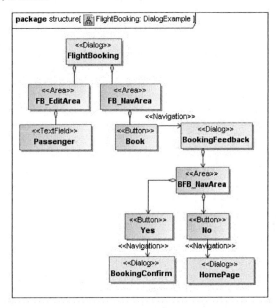

Fig. 4: Example application PIM for flight-booking

On the basis of such a PIM a generator for the target-architecture *Web 2.0* can automatically create an AJAX based application (PSM/PSI). Figure 5 shows the exemplary flight-booking as a Web 2.0 application: The booking-button on the booking-dialog triggers the navigation to the feedback-dialog ("Buchung bestätigen" in German means "Booking confirmation").

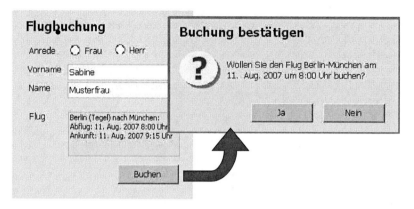

Fig. 5: Flight-booking example as Web 2.0 application

The example introduced above should make the point clear, that modeling an interactive system with the use of UML and the MBUI profile is possible and sufficiently abstract, so that generators can support miscellaneous target-architectures, but is bound to two disadvantages:

a) Due to the high amount of structural details the models tend to become unclear when getting larger.

b) This kind of modeling does not support usability-engineering which takes software-ergonomic requirements into account.

HCI Patterns can, at least partly, be seen as the solution to the second problem. The following chapters will provide a short introduction to HCI Patterns.

3.3 HCI Patterns

HCI Patterns should – just like Design Patterns – provide established solutions for problems that arise during the development of interactive systems, that is to say, causing a transfer of knowledge [Borc00]. The tasks can be derived from software-ergonomic requirements, such as controllability, self-descriptiveness, and conformity with user expectations [ISO9241].

Therefore, the basis for many HCI Patterns are corresponding principles of the Usability Engineering, for instance *Recognise Not Recall*. The HCI Pattern *The Wizard* [Welie07] points to the Usability Principle *User Guidance* (Visibility). [Folm07] shows the connection between heuristics and HCI Patterns, using the example of the application-domain computer game (s. fig. 6).

Table 1: patterns identified and organized	
Nielsen's heuristics	**Pattern name**
Visibility of system status (4)	Game Progress, Instant Replay, Closed Captioning, Visual Saves.
User control and freedom (3)	Free look, Pause, Skip Cut scene.
Error prevention (5)	Auto Save, Control Assistance. Plavaround. Slow.

Fig. 6: Heuristics and HCI Patterns according to [Folm06]

Besides the application-domains HCI Patterns can also be classified by other criteria [Dear00], e.g. by [Mahe01]:

1. Organisational Process Patterns,
2. High-Level Specification Patterns and
3. Detailed Design Patterns.

Whereas the first two kinds of patterns focus on complex cases and superordinate aspects, e.g. the culture of users, the *Detailed Design Patterns* rather address the concrete implementation. Such patterns can be described by "normal" Design Patterns [Went06] to some extent, such as the *Undo-Pattern* [Tidw05] can be described using the patterns *Memento* and *Command* [Gamm95].

By now there are numerous HCI Pattern libraries, some of them are publicly available over the web, e.g.[Weli04] or [HCIP]. The possibilities of pattern-description reaches from textual notation to the use of formal languages, such as the XML. As a language-standard for describing patterns the *Pattern Language Markup Language* (PLML) [Finc03], which covers the areas typical for patterns, is available. For example it contains a description for pattern name, problems, context, forces (strengths, weaknesses, opportunities, threats), solution, synopsis, example, rationale, confidence, and author.

4 HCI Patterns in the MDA-context

4.1 Model-based HCI Patterns

In principle, HCI Patterns can be expressed formally, using UML Profiles or MOF compliant languages – at least most for the *Detailed Design Patterns.*

Within the MBUI project several patterns were modeled in the UML. Figure 7 shows the HCI Pattern *Feedback,* showing a dialog window with three buttins (yes, no, and cancel). Navigation interactions are assigned to these buttons, so that a user can navigate to other dialog windows with the help of a feedback window (positive result or negative result) or back to the triggering dialog (cancel).[3]

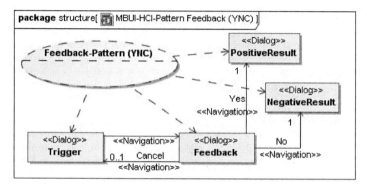

Fig. 7: MBUI HCI Pattern Feedback

The feedback-pattern is flexible to a certain degree, since it lets the UI developer choose, whether the cancel button should be present or not, so that an intentional choice can be made.

figure 8.shows how the pattern can be applied to the flight booking example.

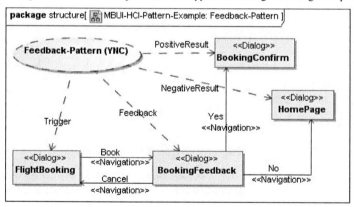

Fig. 8: Application of the feedback HCI Pattern

---

3   The foundation for this are navigation-models, which are known for some time in Usability Engineering [Petr00].

Using the pattern helps the UI developer to make the right decisions and to meet requirements for the user interface, specially with interaction techniques like navigation. This addresses problem (b) mentioned above (s. chapter 3.2): In the original version the dialog window consists only of a yes and a no button, but offered no cancel interaction. The feedback pattern prevents this fault because it suggests a cancel button.

The new navigation models are also called PIMs and can be transformed to PSMs or PSIs. The feedback dialog, generated from MBUI models (PIM), now offers the user three navigational interactions (yes, no, cancel, s. fig. 9).

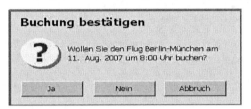

Fig. 9: Generated feedback dialog with yes, no and cancel buttons

At first glance the example of a forgotten cancel button may seem trivial and unimportant, so there seems to by a reason to cast doubt on HCI Patterns. However, the following arguments should be considered:

a) When it comes to usability, every detail counts. Since the user has to cope with the UI constantly (and maybe for a long time) and performs interactions with serious consequences.

b) The quantity and quality of ergonomic requirements make it necessary that the user interface designer and the software developers get an appropriate environment helping them with style guides (and HCI patterns), but still maintains the flexibility for the development of special and individual design solutions.

If properly defined and used, MBUI HCI Patterns can make a positive contribution: With every pattern important details are made available, whereupon the UI developer is still flexible and has to make individual decisions. This means that there is a transfer of knowledge and experience: Proven HCI solutions and best practices can quickly be incorporated in development processes without technical details distracting from the main subject of user interface design. In conjunction with a MDA tool for the automatic UI code generation the development team can leverage on the advantages of HCI patterns.

Finally, the introduced model based concepts for the development of interactive systems should be embedded in an HCI development process.

4.2 Model based HCI development process

A suitable development process was defined during the MBUI research project in order to use the ISO 13407 in conjunction with model based HCI patterns (s. Fig 9). The MBUI process incorporates MDA specific elements into the *Human Centred Design* process of the ISO 13407. The phases of this *MBUI Design Process* are:

1. Planning of the MBUI Design Process,
2. OOA: Analysis and specification of the context of use (CIM),
3. OOA: Modeling of user and organizational requirements (PIM),

4a. OOD: Transformation of PIMs (model to model, M2M) and additional modeling / user
    interface design on the level of the PSMs,

4b. OOP: Transformation (model to code, M2C) and manual programming (PSI)

5. Evaluation of user interface designs with model driven testing and user oriented techniques

The MBUI generator is developed by the platform project, that also provides the UML profile, the patterns, the transformations and the MBUI tool chain. Fig. 10 show the *MBUI Design Process* in principle.

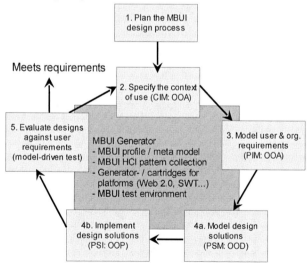

Figure 10: MBUI Design Process

5. Conclusion

HCI modeling and HCI patterns can be used in conjunction with model driven development and OMG's MDA. However some conceptual and tool oriented aspects should be taken into consideration. Also the qualification level is very important: The persons involved must manage the high level of formalization and abstractness, e.g. user interface designer, usability engineer, software architect. The UI models must be exactly and precisely specified in a formal language.

Nevertheless, the Model Based User Interface (MBUI) approach has several advantages like the possibility of technologically (and platform) independent UI concepts and designs that enables the development team to implement user interfaces for old and new platforms and technologies with reduced effort because of the code generation. More time can be spent on software ergonomic aspects and as a result reusable models are created. Technological innovation cycles can easier be "survived" with this approach.

The MDA idea of the separation of user interface design and the technological platform is possible for the HCI development in order to produce software on a professional level. But further work is necessary to leverage the advantages of model based user interface design and usability engineering, e.g. the analysis and consideration of other approaches like Contextual Design [Baye98]. Also the possibilities and limitations of the formalization and modeling in conjunction with usability principles, heuristics and standards is to be examined, e.g. [Cons99], [Shne97], ISO9241]. Related work like [Forb06] shows that model based user interfaces design has a bright future.

References

[Baye98]   H. Bayer, K. Holtzblatt.: *Contextual Design*. Morgan Kaufmann Publishers, 1998

[Bayl98]   E. Bayle, R. Bellamy, G. Casaday, T. Erickson, S. Fincher, B. Grinter, B. Gross, D. Lehder, H. Marmolin, B. Moore, C. Potts, G. Skousen, J. Thomas: *Putting it all together: towards a pattern language for interaction design. SGICHI Bulletin*, 30(1), 1998, S. 17-23

[Blan04]   K. Blankenhorn: *A UML Profile for GUI Layout*, University of Applied Sciences, Furtwangen, Diplomarbeit, 2004

[Borc00]   J. Borchers: Interaction Design Patterns: *Twelve Theses, Position Paper*. In: *Workshop:Pattern Languages for Interaction Design*. Proceedings CHI 2000. 2-3 April, The Hague, Netherlands, 2000

[Brad98]   M. Bradac, B. Fletcher: *A Pattern Language for Developing Form Style Windows*. In: R. Martin, D. Riehle, F. Buschmann (Hrsg.): *Pattern Languages of Program Design*. Addison-Wesley Longman, Reading, MA, 1998, S. 347-357

[Ceri03]   S. Ceri, P. Fraternali, A. Bongio, M. Brambilla, S. Comai, M. Matera:

Designing Data-Intensive Web Applications. The Morgan Kaufmann Series in Data Management Systems, 2003 (s. auch Webml Research Group: The Web Modelling Language. http://www.webml.org)

[Cons99] L. Constantine, L. Lockwood: Software for Use. A practical Guide to the Models and Methods of Usage-Centered Design. Addison-Wesley, 1999

[Cora96] T. Coram, J. Lee: *Experiences -- A Pattern Language for User Interface Design*. In: Pattern Languages of Program Design, Proceedings, 1996

[Dear00] A. Dearden: *Patterns and Participation: The relevance of Christopher Alexander's ideas for HCI*. In: Proceedings of the BCS HCI Group/IFIP WG13.2 Workshop on HCI Patterns, London, UK, 2000

[Finc03] S. Fincher: *Perspective on HCI Patterns: Concepts and tools (introducing PLML)*. In: Interfaces (56), British HCI Group, CHI 2003 Workshop Report, 2003, S. 27-28

[Folm06] E. Folmer: *Usability Patterns in Games*. Futureplay 2006 Conference, London, Ontario, Canada, 3. Oct. 2006 (http://www.eelke.com)

[Forb06] P. Forbig, D. Reichert: : *Modellbasierte Entwicklung von modellbasierten Werkzeugen*. In: [Fieb06]

[Gamm95] E. Gamma, R. Helm, R., Johnson, J. Vlissides: *Design Patterns: Elements of Reusable Object Oriented Software*, Addison-Wesley, Reading, MA., 1995

[Grah03] I. Graham: *A pattern language for web usability*. Addison-Wesley, 2003

[Hart90] H. R. Hartson, A. C. Siochi, D. Hix: The UAN: A User-Oriented Representation for Direct Manipulation Interface Designs, ACM Transactions on Information Systems, Vol. 8, No. 3, July 1990, Pages 181-203

[HCIP] http://www.hcipatterns.org

[ISO13407] ISO/DIS 13407 *Human-centred design processes for interactive systems*. ISO, 1999

[ISO9241] ISO 9241-110:2006: *Ergonomics of human-system interaction -- Part 110: Dialogue principles*. ISO, 2006

[Koch01] N. Koch: *Software Engineering for Adaptive Hypermedia Systems: Reference Model, Modeling Techniques and Development Process*. Diss., Ludwig-Maximilians-University Munich, 2001

[Lang94] D. Lange: *An Object-Oriented Design Method for Hypermedia Information Systems*. In: Proceedings of the 27th Hawaii International Conference on System Science, S. 366-375, 1994

[Mahe01] M. J. Mahemoff, L. J. Johnston: *Usability Pattern Languages: the "Language" Aspect*. In: M. Hirose (Hrsg), Human-Computer Interaction: Interact '01, Tokyo, Japan, , IOS Press, S. 350-358

[MDA] Object Management Group (OMG): *MDA Guide*. Version 1.0.1,

	omg/2003-06-01, June 2003
[MOF]	Object Management Group (OMG): *MOF 2.0 – Meta Object Facility Core Specification*. Version 2.0. Adopted Specification, ptc/03-10-04, Oct. 2003
[Myer92]	Myers, B. and Rosson, M. B.: *Survey on User Interface Programming*, in Proceedings of CHI92 Conference, ACM., 1992
[Nune01]	N. J. Nunes: *Object Modeling for User-Centered Development and User Interface Design: The Wisdom Approach*, Universidade da Madeira, Diss., 2001
[Petr00]	R. Petrasch: *Development of Ergonomic Software: Transformation from Requirements to Features using a Web Application's Navigation Space as an Example*. In: Conference Proceedings, CONQUEST 2000 –Conference on Quality Engineering in Software Technology", ASQF, Sept. 2000, S. 118-127
[Petr06]	R. Petrasch, O. Meimberg: *Model Driven Architecture. Eine praxisorientierte Einführung in die MDA*. dpunkt Verlag, 2006
[Phan00]	C. Phanouriou: *UIML: A Device-Independent User Interface Markup Language*. Diss., Virginia Polytechnic Institute and State University, USA, 2000 (http://www.uiml.org)
[QVT]	Object Management Group (OMG): *Ouery/Views/Transformation* (QVT). Version 1.0, formal/08-04-03, 2008
[Shne97]	Shneiderman, B.: Designing the User Interface: Strategies for Effective Human-Computer Interaction. 3. Auflage, Addison-Wesley, 1997
[Silv02]	P. Pinheiro da Silva: *Object Modelling of interactive systems: The UMLi approach*, University of Manchester, Diss., 2002
[Silv03]	P. Pinheiro da Silva, N. W. Paton: *User Interface Modeling in UMLi*. IEEE Software, July/Aug. 2003, S. 62-69
[Tidw99]	J. Tidwell: *COMMON GROUND: A Pattern Language for Human-Computer Interface Design*. http://www.mit.edu/~jtidwell/common_ground_onefile.html, 1999
[Tidw05]	J. Tidwell: *Designing Interfaces*. O'Reilly Media, Sebastopol, USA, 2005
[Tidw98]	J. Tidwell: *Interaction Patterns*. In: Pattern Languages of Program Design,Proceedings, Monticello, IL., USA, 1998
[UML]	Object Management Group (OMG): *UML 2.1.1 – Unified Modeling Language* (UML) Superstructure. Version 2.2., formal/09-02-02, 2009
[Welie03]	M. Van Welie, G. C. Van Der Veer: *Pattern Languages*. In: M. Rauterberg, M Menozzi, J Wesson (Hrsg.): *Interaction Design: Structure and Organization*, INTERACT 2003, . IOS Press, Zürich, Switzerland, September 2003
[Went06]	I. Wentzlaff, M. Specker: *Pattern Based Development of User Friendly Web Applications*. ACM ICWE'06 Workshops, Palo Alto, CA, USA,

10.-14. Juli 2006

[Welie07]   M. Van Welie: *Web Design Patterns*. http://www.welie.com/patterns (Stand: 1.7.2007)

On-the-fly MDA application modelling using Executable and Translatable UML

Ing. Otto ZELEZNIK, doc. Ing. Zdenek HAVLICE, CSc.
[1]Dept. of Computers and Informatics
Faculty of Electrical Engineering and Informatics,
Technical University of Kosice, Letna 9
042 00 Kosice
Slovak Republic

Abstract

This paper presents a proposal of a method for MDA based "on-the-fly" modelling of Musical Real Time Applications which are implemented using the Executable and Translatable UML approach (xtUML). Since we want to implement a real-time application which requires certain real-time Quality of Service (QoS) properties as well as meeting the main requirement of proposed method which is user/architect ability of application model modification in real-time during execution, we prefer to split the overall system into two parts. The first part will be the implementation environment – the programmer/provider system which will provide for the runtime environment of the user model itself - modelled using xtUML on-the-fly. The necessity of such system separation is only required due to the fact that modelling easiness and performance requirement plays an important role for user as an architect of his model. In such proposed architecture the user has the advantage of separating concerns in his modelling the way he does not need to care about the implementation environment neither about any specific QoS properties of the target platform which in the end means easiness of modelling and good real-time performance.

1 Introduction

The modern era brings among us an evolution of our lives in every aspect. This is particularly true in the area of applying new methods in software architectures design especially focused on embedded systems used for sound and signal processing, musical production and musical real-time applications. These kinds of applications can be considered as specific software-hardware "musical instruments" as they provide the user/artist for creating or altering the musical piece in real time – while the artist is performing his show. We can consider this application kind as an information system since it processes information in form of sound and its properties.

The Musical Real-Time Applications usually consists of a combination of a specific signal processing software which is implemented on a viable hardware platform whereas each part has specific properties and requirements (QoS, good real-time response). Since the fundamental purpose of these applications is sound effects execution based on a command query from the user, the implementation platform is usually based on a well designed embedded system. A powerful Digital Signal Processor is usually a core of such system cooperating with various peripherals, sensors, actuators and converters. The converters perform environment signal conversion (input and output sound in our case) into the digital domain and vice versa, the mentioned DSP processor then realises a signal alteration following the user commands and settings using various signal processing methods [1] which are not to be described in detail here due to rather limited paper scope. Sensors and actuators on the other hand gather and scatter the controlling user input commands and output feedback providing user with various status information necessary to generate a correct input commands within the application. The figure 1 depicts an example overall architecture of the Musical Real-Time Application defined in the above paragraph.

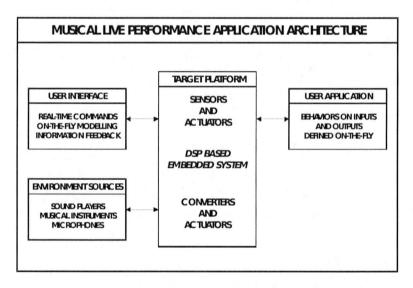

Fig. 1 – Typical architecture of a Musical Real Time Application

Our application kind covers for various embedded systems devices, such as sound effectors with real-time control [2], musical samples generators, variable filters, etc.

2 Standard and current approaches to our application type modelling

Since the user – artist expects to achieve only the best performance when using such tools, there are two major and most important properties of these applications. One of them is a very good real-time response on user commands, the other one is the ability to configure the sound alteration scheme (algorithms) as freely as possible, e.g. the ability to model what the system has to do with the sound in real time. Mentioned aspects of such applications are nowadays solved rather in limited measure. Since the implementation and design (based usually on embedded systems) are rather time and programmer's resources consuming, the usual up-to-date solutions only offer the user a very limited range of configurability of applicable signal processing algorithms and meet only minimal ability for modification in real time.

The main reason of such limitations in standard implementations is a need for laborious hand-manner approach when designing embedded systems with focus on very good real time response. Such systems require careful evaluation of all requested parameters of the application as well as evaluation of the abilities of the target platform. Special care must be taken on the viewpoint of the Platform Model (PM) / Platform Specific Model (PSM) so to meet all Quality of Service (QoS) requirements requested by the Application as well as given by the Target Platform. The application must be measured from various viewpoints considering the resources of the target hardware architecture such as computational power of the core processor, various specific properties of memory types, memory sizes, communication channels between peripherals, language types and evaluation of mixed or hand-optimised programming need for critical parts of the system (OS scheduler, peripheral drivers, etc). A more detailed analysis on various aspects of embedded systems design is demonstrated in [3], [7]. Such design methods perform good in achieving very good real time response of the system, they also however causes nearly unsolvable difficulties when trying to implement the user's ability to modify user parts of application in real time - on-the-fly, all this without a need for programmer/architect or even recompiling whole project.

One of the ways how to deal with cases where modifiability on-the-fly is essential is to approach modelling using MDA and Executable and Translatable UML (xtUML).

3 Our MDA with xtUML approach to our application type modelling

MDA is defined by the OMG group [4], [5], [6] as modelling technique particularly focused on separating concerns while designing applications and systems. It basically defines three distinctive models used for various aspects description: PIM (Platform Independent Model), PM (Platform Model) and PSM (Platform Specific Model). Each mentioned model describes system through a specific viewpoint such as it separates concerns of the platform and the application from each other. The first mentioned model (PIM) characterises functioning and structure of the system with complete abstraction from the platform where the application suppose to be   implemented. By employing such approach we can achieve complete separation of concerns and as a result the user – architect gains much better portability of the application between various platforms and architectures while meeting all requested properties, contents of the application and its behaviour as well. PIM model together with the PM model then server as base for transformation into PSM model, which includes all implementation specifications of the given hardware platform where the application has to be executed.

Such modelling technique is very beneficial for our application kind and it brings us several advantages. Sound and signal processing technologies are nowadays constantly evolving also in common PC computers. There is a superior trend in using Musical Real Time Application among artistic world as well. The MDA approach in the mentioned applications seems therefore a very spontaneous and valid modelling direction. Such approach assures a very good ability to implement the same model on various platforms – embedded systems as well as the platforms based on PC with operating systems while meeting all requested properties, contents and behaviour defined by models.

To use just the MDA for achieving all of the requested properties in case of our application kind will however be hardly satisfactory. One of the main required properties is the on-the-fly modifiability of the PIM user model. To implement such system only within the MDA prospects would be rather awkward especially due to unrealistic recompiling of the whole system in real time. We therefore propose a method which uses Executable and Translatable UML as the in-between layer within the PIM model. The resulting transformed PIM model is executed via xtUML specification within already defined architecture through the PM and PSM models, which are designed to execute the xtUML PIM model in real time with a very good real time response.

The xtUML standard [8], [9] is defined so that it can design comprehensible model for an application without any knowledge about how the internal structure of the software is made. This fact makes the xtUML a well abstract tool which elegantly solves also our application kind modelling. Not to mention there is a possibility to implement such xtUML model on various already existing platforms also for verification purposes.

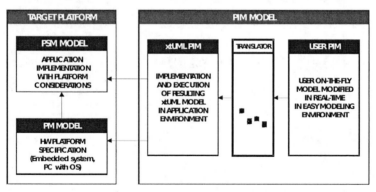

Fig.2 – Proposed MDA with xtUML based model for Musical Real Time Applications

The figure 2 presents a proposal of modelling technique of our application kind using the MDA approach with xtUML models. Due to the need of modifiable user PIM model in real time, a middle layer is embedded in between the user PIM and the resulting xtUML PIM which provides for a transformation of the user PIM model into the xtUML specification. The user PIM model is rather specified in a so-called Easy Modelling Environment. The resulting xtUML model is directly executed on a target platform.

Such transformation "middle-man" allows the user – artist skip unnecessary learning of the xtUML standard and at the same time allows achieve more important aspect of modelling the user PIM model - using very straightforward and easily understandable modelling environment (for example graphically specified). Such environment is to be especially designed with focus on Musical Real Time Applications specifications with high focus on ergonomics and time-savings while designing the model. The mentioned transformation middle-man as well as other parts of the proposed modelling method is subject for further research included in my ongoing PhD thesis.

The advantages arising from the above mentioned transformation are multiple. One of them is the ability to simulate and verify [7] resulting xtUML model due its execution with addition of error feedback to the user about correctness of his model.

4 Case study

To help understand and evaluate the needs and properties of the Easy Modelling Environment as well as the specifications of the model-to-model transformation into xtUML we propose to further study a real application case. The modelling environment for digital effector application with real time modelling ability is to be designed. The application should also implement the artificial intelligence methods which should help improve ergonomics and easiness of the user PIM modelling process. The information such as musical genre, beats-per-minute, gathered from the musical material are to be used in mentioned AI methods as basis for modelling process optimization. As for the target platform we suggest to use a combination of two complementary platforms. An embedded system will provide for sound alteration algorithms execution as well as musical properties information analysis. The PC platforms based on standard operating systems will provide for the Easy Modelling Environment of the user PIM models allowing to use even multiple parallel-executed environments at the same time. This would allow more users - artists to perform at the same time thus creating more complex performance advancing creativity possibilities in Musical Real Time Applications. The scheme on figure 3 briefly describes such architecture example.

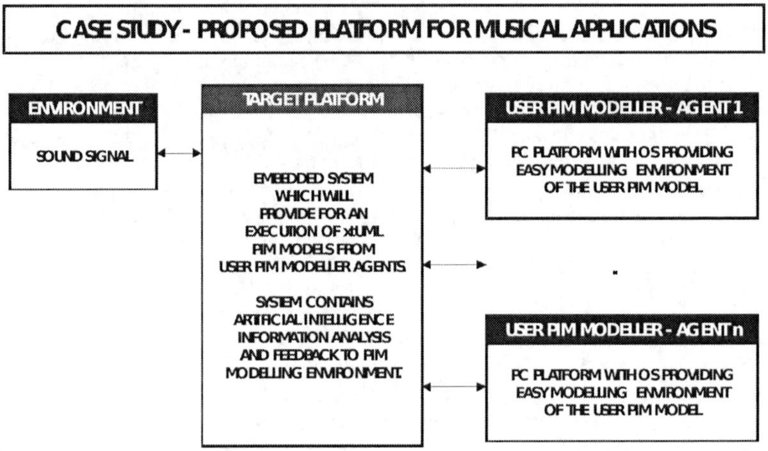

CASE STUDY - PROPOSED PLATFORM FOR MUSICAL APPLICATIONS

ENVIRONMENT	TARGET PLATFORM	USER PIM MODELLER - AGENT 1
SOUND SIGNAL	EMBEDDED SYSTEM WHICH WILL PROVIDE FOR AN EXECUTION OF xtUML PIM MODELS FROM USER PIM MODELLER AGENTS	PC PLATFORM WITH OS PROVIDING EASY MODELLING ENVIRONMENT OF THE USER PIM MODEL
	SYSTEM CONTAINS ARTIFICIAL INTELLIGENCE INFORMATION ANALYSIS AND FEEDBACK TO PIM MODELLING ENVIRONMENT	USER PIM MODELLER - AGENT n
		PC PLATFORM WITH OS PROVIDING EASY MODELLING ENVIRONMENT OF THE USER PIM MODEL

Fig.3 – Proposed case study platform for Musical Real Time Applications

5 Conclusion

This paper presents a MDA approach with use of the Executable and Translatable UML for modelling Musical Real Time Applications with special focus on the modifiability of the user PIM model on-the-fly. The core idea of the proposed method is to separate user PIM model from the implementation PIM model of the rest of the application and a method is suggested for modelling the user PIM model using a specific Easy Modelling Environment with high focus on ergonomics and easiness of the model design. Such modelling environment should facilitate time-saving while modelling as well as be very understandable in the definition to the user – artist. Resulting xtUML PIM model is achieved by transformation of such user PIM model and is afterwards executed on the target platform.

Such method also guarantees various advantages over standard modelling methods and approaches. One of the advantages is easy portability over various platforms enabling to use the embedded systems as well as common PC platforms for execution. The major advantage is however the ability to modify the user PIM model on-the-fly in real time.

Acknowledgement

This work was supported by VEGA Grant No. 1/0350/08 Knowledge-Based Software Life Cycle and Architectures.

References

[1] Lathi, B. P., Signal Processing & Linear Systems. Oxford University Press, New York (1998)

[2] Pioneer Pro DJ, EFX-1000 performance effector. Pioneer Pro DJ, http://www.pioneerprodj.com/dj-equipment/effects/efx-1000.asp, 2006

[3] O.Zeleznik, Z.Havlice, Software Architectures for Real-Time Embedded Applications for broadcasting. 10th International Conference on Information System Implementation and Modeling ISIM'07, 2nd International Workshop on Formal Models WFM'07, Hradec nad Moravici, 2007

[4] OMG, Model driven architecture guide v1.0.1. http://www.omg.org/mda, 2003

[5] OMG, UML 2.0 OCL specification. http://www.omg.org/ocl, 2003

[6] OMG, UML profile for modelling QoS and fault tolerant characteristics and mechanisms. OMG adopted specification, 2004

[7] J.DeAntoni, J.P.Babau, A MDA-based approach for real time embedded systems simulation. Ninth IEEE International Symposium on Distributed Simulations and Real-Time Applications, 2005

[8] S.J.Mellor, M.J.Balcer, Executable UML: A Foundation for Model-Driven Architecture, Addison-Wesley Professional, 2002

[9] S.J.Mellor, Executable and Translatable UML, Embedded Systems Design (www.embedded.com), 2003

83

An Application of the MDSE Principles in IIS*Case

Ivan Lukovic[1], Sonja Ristic[2], Slavica Aleksic[3], Aleksandar Popovic[4]

[1][2][3] University of Novi Sad
Faculty of Technical Sciences
Trg D. Obradovica 6
Novi Sad
Serbia
[4] University of Montenegro
Faculty of Science
George Washington bb, Podgorica
Montenegro

Abstract

A Model-Driven (MD) approach to the system development increases the importance and power of models by shifting the focus from programming to modeling activities. The models may be used as primary artifacts in constructing software which means that a code is generated from models. Software development tools need to automate as many as possible tasks of model construction and transformation requiring for that the smallest amount of human interaction.

Integrated Information Systems Case Tool (IIS*Case) is a software development tool aimed to provide the information system (IS) design and generating executable application prototypes. In the paper we consider an applying of the MDSE principles in IIS*Case. A generator of the executable program code for target program environments and an SQL generator for various target DBMSs are based on a technology independent IS model designed in IIS*Case. In the paper we present and briefly discuss the IIS*Case technology independent concepts and models.

1 Introduction

For more than ten years, software industry has been using models that allow a system to be precisely described at the appropriate abstraction level without unnecessary details. The main assumption of the model-driven approach to software system development is that software systems of large complexity can only be designed and maintained if the level of abstraction is considerably higher than that of programming languages. By means of models, semantics in an application domain can be precisely specified using terms and concepts the end-users are familiar with. The focus of software development is shifted from the technology domain toward the problem domain. A complex system

85

may consist of many interrelated models organized through different layers of abstraction. Since we assume that computers operate at the very low level of abstraction, those models need to be transformed into the languages that the target platform can understand and perform. Therefore, a chain of transformations should be completed starting from an initial model at the highest level of abstraction, through the less abstract models, and resulting in an executable program code that represents a model at the lowest level of abstraction. Accordingly, we may expect that present software development tools should automate as many as possible tasks of model construction and transformations requiring for that the smallest amount of human interaction.

Integrated Information Systems Case Tool (IIS*Case) is a software tool aimed to provide the information system (IS) design and generating executable application prototypes. Its development is spanned through a number of research projects lasting for several years, in which the authors of the paper are actively involved. Our main motives for the development of IIS*Case were (i) to provide the generation of db schemas and fully operational application prototypes without manual coding of programs, or even without knowing the syntax of a particular domain-specific or general-purpose programming language; (ii) to enable designers and end-users to model semantics of an application domain in a natural way, using the concepts they are familiar with; (iii) to preserve the formal correctness of the transformation process of initial designers' specifications into the target program code; and (iv) to define a comprehensive methodological approach that supports usage of IIS*Case not only in small, but also in large-scale projects.

In our approach we strictly differentiate between the specification of a system and its implementation on a particular platform. By means of IIS*Case, modeling is performed at the high abstraction level, because a designer creates an IS model without specifying any implementation details. Such a model may be classified as a Platform-Independent Model (PIM) of the MDA pattern. IIS*Case currently contains an SQL generator for various target Database Management Systems (DBMSs). Also, a generator of the executable application prototypes for a selected target program environment is under development. The source specification for both of the generators is a technology independent IS model created in IIS*Case. In the paper we briefly describe technology independent concepts and models embedded into the IIS*Case tool V.6.6, and argue that IIS*Case is based on the IS development approach that shares the same basic ideas the MDA approach relies on. We also outline a model-to-model transformation from the domain-specific model of a system to the abstract relational model, provided by IIS*Case. The generation of SQL scripts for different target DBMSs is presented as an example of model-to-code transformation embedded into IIS*Case.

2 IIS*Case – A Brief Overview

Modeling process in IIS*Case is raised to the level that is closer to the users without an advanced knowledge of the information system and database design.

Our intention is that IIS*Case should provide:

- a simple and natural way for defining the initial set of attributes and data constraints of various kinds;

- an intelligent support during the design process;
- a cooperative work of designers in reaching the most appropriate solutions; and
- saving designers' working time and effort, due to the fact that a majority of the tasks are automated. Therefore, a designer may devote his/her time and power to analysis and modeling of system processes and business rules.

Initially, IIS*Case was developed to support an automated database schema design, based on the concepts that are close to the end-users from a problem domain. A central IIS*Case concept is the form type, which is an abstraction used to model the structure and constraints of various business documents ([1], [8], [14]). Relational database schemas are generated using the form type specifications. IIS*Case is based on a methodology of gradual integration of independently designed subschemas into a database schema ([8], [12], [14], [15]). Therefore, we believe that an IS model created by IIS*Case may be classified as a PIM model.

Currently, IIS*Case comprises tools for:

- conceptual modeling of a database schema;
- automated design of relational database subschemas in the 3rd normal form;
- automated integration of relational database subschemas;
- automated detection of constraint collisions;
- generating XML specifications of an IS;
- full implementation of database schemas under different target DBMSs, by using its own SQL Generator; and
- conceptual modeling of transaction programs, and business applications of an IS.

We also define a methodological approach to the application of IIS*Case in the software development process. By this approach, the software development process provided by IIS*Case is, in general, evolutive and incremental. We believe that it enables an efficient and continuous development of a software system, as well as an early delivery of software prototypes that can be easily upgraded or amended according to the new or changed users' requirements. Detailed information about IIS*Case may be found in several authors' references, as well as in [1], [7], [10]. A case study illustrating main features of IIS*Case and the methodological aspects of its usage is given in [8], [10], and accordingly we do not repeat the same explanations here.

By the MDA approach, the system modeling is raised to the higher abstraction level, by differentiating between the PIM and the Platform-Specific Models (PSM). PIMs are fully independent of any implementation platform, while PSMs contain information specific for a selected implementation platform ([11], [13]). A complex system may consist of many interrelated models organized through different abstraction layers. A PSM model at one layer may have the role of a PIM model as a source for further transformations into another layer. In general, it is possible to have a chain of transformations that can be completed starting from an initial PIM model and resulting in the executable program code. Nowadays, there are various software tools that provide such transformations .

There are similarities between MDA and the approach IIS*Case relies on. By means of

IIS*Case, a designer creates only PIM models, because they are free of any implementation details ([8],[10]). Various project team members or stakeholders have their own views on the system. In this context, a notion of the *view* ([6],[11]) is a single representation of the system specified by a "language" comprehensible to the view consumers. Such a "language" is named viewpoint ([6], [11]). A particular view may be expressed in an abstract way using the concepts and the structuring rules of the selected viewpoint. The concepts provided by IIS*Case are semantically rich enough, and it is allowed their grouping into not necessarily disjoint subsets. These subsets of concepts and the rules for their structuring can be considered as the different viewpoints. A designer can create various views based on these viewpoints. Some of the views that can be created by IIS*Case are the following ones:

- layout and functional properties of screen forms of the user interface (UI);
- business application diagrams (Fig. 2);
- relational database schemas;
- closure graph diagrams of a database schema (Fig. 3); etc.

Some of the aforementioned views may be classified as MDA PIM models, while the others may be classified as MDA PSM models. Characterizing a model as a PIM or PSM depends on the selected platform and may be relative . For example, database schema expressed by the relational data model could be seen as PSM model, since relational technology is used. On the other hand, one can say that it is a PIM model since it is independent of a particular relational DBMS. PSMs are created from PIM models by transformations performed mainly by software tools. It is preferable that the transformation process is fully automated, with as minimum as possible human interaction. The transformations combine a PIM with additional information to produce a PSM. The existing, as well as the future development of IIS*Case is oriented towards providing the transformations of platform independent views into a larger number of platform specific views.

3 Technology Independent Concepts in IIS*Case

The set of IIS*Case concepts that are technology independent can be split into two disjoint subsets:

- fundamental (common) concepts that include: domain, attribute, function, package, and event; and
- application specific concepts that include: project, application system, business application, form type, and component type.

All the designers' specifications of an IS model created by IIS*Case belong to an IIS*Case *project* . Each project is organized as a tree structure of *application systems*, where each application system may contain an arbitrary number of form types. A *form type* is the main modeling concept in IIS*Case. Each form type is an abstraction of business documents, and therefore screen or report forms utilized by the end-users of the IS. In the traditional approaches to the IS design, database schema design precedes the specification of screen or report forms of transaction programs. On the contrary, in IIS*Case a designer the first specifies screen or report forms, and indirectly, creates an initial set of attributes and constraints. The set of form types is a platform independent view onto the IS from the end-user perspective. IIS*Case uses the set of form types to generate the relational database schema, and its closure graph . In this way, by creating form types, a designer specifies: (i) a future database schema, (ii) functional properties of future transaction programs, (iii) and a look of the end-user interface, all at the same time.

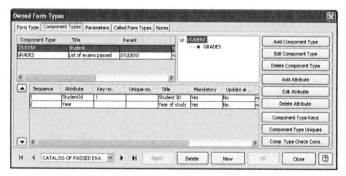

Figure 1. The IIS*Case form for specification of a form type

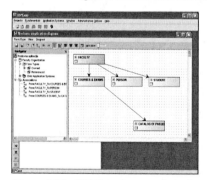

Figure 2. The IIS*Case diagram of a business application

Figure 3. The IIS*Case closure graph diagram of a db schema

A form type is a hierarchical structure of form type components (Fig. 1). Each component type is identified by its name within the scope of a form type, and has non-empty sets of attributes and keys, a possibly empty set of unique constraints, and a specification of the check constraint. A set of allowed database operations must be associated with each component type. The set of allowed operations is a subset of the set of "standard" operations {*retrieve, insert, update, delete*}. If the *update* operation is associated with a component type, the set of updatable attributes of the component type must be also specified. In addition, each attribute of a component type may be marked as mandatory or optional.

Each attribute of a component type is selected from a global set of all information system attributes. According to the well-known universal relation scheme assumption present in the relational data model, the attributes are globally identified only by their names. IIS*Case imposes strict rules for specifying attributes and their domains, and for specifying component type attributes.

IIS*Case is planned to provide the generation of a program code of transaction programs and applications that are executed over a database. A form type is a source for the generation of a sole transaction program and its screen or report form. In order to enable formal specification of functionalities concerning relationships (so called "calls") between generated screen forms, i.e. transaction programs, a concept named *business application* is introduced. The scope of each business application created in IIS*Case is an application system, because any business application belongs to exactly one application system. Specifying the form types must precede the design of a business application, because the specification of a business application in IIS*Case comprises a structure of the selected form types (Fig. 2). Therefore, a business application specification is a source for the generation of a program code that covers calls between generated transaction programs, i.e. their forms, and a synchronization of their behavior.

The union of the sets of form types of a selected application system and all its application subsystems, alongside with the set of its business applications represents a technology independent model of the real system being observed. The process of generating a relational database schema of an application system is the first in the chain of model transformations implemented in IIS*Case. In the following section, we briefly present it in order to illustrate one of the IIS*Case model-to-model transformations.

4 A Transformation of a Project Specification into a Formal Database Schema Specification

The form type structuring rules provide an automatic inference of the set of attributes and relational database constraints. The initial set of constraints, inferred from a form type, consists of: a set of functional dependencies F; a set of non-functional dependencies NF; a set of special functional dependencies F_u; and a set of null value constraints N_c. The sets F, NF and F_u are defined in [12] and [14]. These constraints are later processed by the synthesis algorithm in the process of a database schema design. The steps of a database schema design process in the IIS*Case environment are presented and illustrated in detail on a case study in [8]. Accordingly, IIS*Case transforms a technology independent model based on the concepts of form types and application systems into a relational database schema satisfying 3NF, which is a system model that depends on the relational technology. From this point of view, it is a technology specific model. It is obtained by a model-to-model transformation from the domain-specific model to the abstract relational model (Fig. 4).

A designer interactively controls the process of the relational database schema generation, giving the necessary additional information. Those information are combined with the technology independent model that is automatically transformed into a relational

90

database schema (Fig. 4). A log file containing the records about the transformation process is also generated.

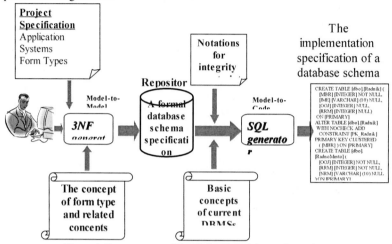

Figure 4. One segment of the chain of model transformations

We believe that our approach to the database schema design process and the appropriate model-to-model transformations has a number of innovations. One of the main ones concerns database schema integration process. By this, we allow an independent and incremental design of segments of a database schema. Those segments we call subschemas. A subschema may represent a database specification of only one application system or it may be the result of the integration of a set of subschemas. By integrating independently designed subschemas, IIS*Case produces the database schema. The process of independent design of subschemas may lead to collisions in expressing the real world constraints and business rules. If the collisions exist, at least one subschema is formally not consistent with the database schema. Programs made over an inconsistent subschema do not guarantee safe database updates. Therefore, IIS*Case uses specialized algorithms to check the consistency of constraints embedded in a database schema and the corresponding subschemas. IIS*Case generates two types of reports: reports on database schema design process and reports on detected collisions. Resolving collisions may lead to producing a new database schema. The database schema integration process, alongside with the collision detection algorithms is presented in [10], [14], and [15].

The generated relational database schema contains all the relation scheme keys, domain and null value constrains, unique constrains, as well as referential and inverse referential integrity constraints [9]. All the generated schemas are stored in the IIS*Case repository. The specification of the IIS*Case repository is given in [14].

At the same abstraction level, the generated relational database schema may be further transformed into another model. Namely, IIS*Case transforms a relational database schema into the closure graph diagram of a database schema (Fig. 3). This is also an example of a model-to-model transformation that is fully automated.

In the following section, we present the SQL Generator in order to illustrate one of the model-to-code transformations implemented in IIS*Case.

5 IIS*Case SQL Generator

The next step in the transformation chain is a transformation of the relational database schema into SQL scripts for a target DBMS. In this way, a more refined model is obtained, and it is classified as technology specific. In this case, the transformation itself is classified as a model-to-code transformation (Fig. 4).

The input into SQL Generator is a schema stored in the repository. SQL generator produces SQL script files with commands for:

- creating tables;
- creating indexes for primary, alternate and foreign keys;
- creating sequences;
- declaring domain constraints;
- declaring primary and equivalent key constraints;
- declaring CHECK constraints;
- declaring referential integrity constraints; and
- creating triggers, procedures and functions.

SQL Generator is capable of producing scripts for implementing a new database schema, or modify an already existing one in the following three ways: (i) by creating SQL scripts in files only for a later execution, (ii) by creating and immediately executing SQL scripts under a selected database server with an established connection, and (iii) by creating and immediately executing SQL scripts on a selected data source with an established connection via an ODBC driver. In all three cases, generated SQL scripts are stored in one or more files.

SQL Generator provides creation of SQL scripts according to the syntax of:

- ANSI SQL:2003 standard;
- DBMS Microsoft (MS) SQL Server 2000/2005 with Microsoft T-SQL; and
- DBMS Oracle 9i/10g with Oracle PL/SQL.

SQL Generator implements constraints of the following types :

- domain constraints;
- key constraints;
- unique constraints;
- tuple constraints;
- native referential integrity constraints – default, partial, full;
- referential integrity constraints inferred from nontrivial inclusion dependencies – default, partial, and full;
- native inverse referential integrity constraints; and
- inverse referential integrity constraints inferred from nontrivial inclusion dependencies.

Constraints are implemented by the declarative DBMS mechanisms, whenever it is possible. However, the expressivity of declarative mechanisms of commercial DBMSs is usually limited in comparison to ANSI SQL:2003 standard. Therefore, SQL Generator implements a number of constraints through the procedural mechanisms, when it is necessary.

The following types of constraints are implemented by procedural mechanisms [6]:

- native referential integrity constraints;
- referential integrity constraints inferred from nontrivial inclusion dependencies;
- native inverse referential integrity constraints; and
- inverse referential integrity constraints inferred from nontrivial inclusion dependencies.

The process of the procedural implementation of a constraint can be unified. It consists of the following steps:

- specifying a parameterized pattern of the algorithm for a specific DBMS;
- replacing the pattern parameters with real values; and
- generating an SQL script comprising necessary triggers, procedures and functions.

SQL generator enables an efficient and automatic transformation of design specifications into error free SQL specifications utilizing both declarative and procedural SQL mechanisms of a target DBMS. The usage of SQL generator free the developers from manual coding and testing and they can use it even without knowing the syntax of SQL and the procedural language of a target DBMS.

IIS*Case SQL Generator, besides common functions implemented in similar tools, provides:

- the implementation of not only the default but the partial and full referential integrity constraints as well;
- the implementation of the inverse referential integrity constraints;
- validating of selections of input parameter values, analyzing of designer's solutions and issuing warnings if any formal inconsistencies are detected;
- producing triggers that prohibit updates of a relation scheme primary keys if such a rule is specified in the database schema; and
- giving a wider selection of possible actions to preserve database consistency for interrelation constraints.

6 Conclusion

In the paper we presented technology independent concepts of the IIS*Case tool, and some of the model transformations implemented in it. IIS*Case currently provides the design of a database schema, SQL scripts, transaction programs, their screen or report forms, and finally the business applications, in an integrated way. By this, we cover the software modeling process of an IS in a great extent. Modeling of an IS by IIS*Case is performed at a high level of abstraction, but with a usage of the concepts that are domain-specific with respect to the application domain of IS development.

Since MDA is based on UML, the success of applying MDA approach in the design process highly depends on how expressively a domain can be modeled using such a general-purpose modeling language, on a platform-independent level. In our approach we use a domain-specific modeling language, which gives designers a freedom to utilize structures and logic that are specific to the target application domain, and still completely independent of the programming language concepts and syntax. We are aware of the importance of UML as one of the common modeling languages targeted to cover the software development process. However, we also believe that flexibility and ease of use by domain experts may be a significant advantage of the approach presented here. Besides, we believe that our approach and UML can be coupled and applied together in the software development process.

IIS*Case tool, initially, almost twenty years ago, was developed as a CASE tool. An important paradigm shift in the field of software engineering towards model as a first class entity happens at the very beginning of the XXI century. We believe that the conceptual capacities of the IIS*Case tool allow relatively easy evolving to the upcoming software engineering standards. Although we have retained its original name for traditional reasons only, we keep going towards its stepping up to the model-driven approach to the software development.

Further development is oriented to the introduction of new concepts, as well as the enrichment of the existing ones. In this way, new viewpoints will be created, so as to enable specifying various views that may cover some new aspects of the system, such as business process definitions or the system (hardware and software) architecture. Besides, a further research that concerns the model-to-model transformations should also provide the algorithms for generation of XML Schema or object-oriented specifications of a database schema designed in IIS*Case.

Currently, our domain specific language, including IIS*Case platform independent concepts, is based on textual specifications with the first-order logic formulas, and on the repository definition used by the specific GUI oriented tools. In order to raise it at meta-meta abstraction level, our research efforts will also be devoted to utilizing the Meta-Object Facility Specification (MOF).

Acknowledgment

A part of the research presented in this paper was supported by Ministry of Science and Technological Development of Republic of Serbia, Grant TR-13029, Title: *A Development of an Intelligent Environment for the Design and Implementation of Information Systems*.

References

[1]   Aleksic S, Lukovic I, Mogin P, Govedarica M, "A Generator of SQL Schema Specifications", Computer Science and Information Systems (ComSIS), Consortium of Faculties of Serbia and Montenegro, Belgrade, Serbia, ISSN: 1820-0214, Vol. 4, No. 2, 2007, pp. 79-98.

[2]   Bézivin J, "In Search of a Basic Principle for Model-Driven Engineering", Novatica Journal, Special Issue, March-April 2004.

[3]   Booch G, Brown A, Iyengar S, Rumbaugh J, Selic B, "An MDA Manifesto", MDA Journal, May 2004.

[4]   Favre J.M, "Foundations of Model (Driven) (Reverse) Engineering: Models", Dagstahl Seminar Proceedings 4101, 2005.

[5]   Govedarica M, Lukovic I, Mogin P, "Generating XML Based Specifications of Information Systems", Computer Science and Information Systems (ComSIS), Consortium of Faculties of Serbia and Montenegro, Belgrade, Serbia and Montenegro, ISSN: 1820-0214, Vol. 1, No. 1, 2004, pp. 117-140.

[6]   IEEE Std 1471-2000, "IEEE Recommended Practice for Architectural Description of Software-Intensive Systems", Approved 21 September 2000.

[7]   Lukovic I, "Automated Relational Database Subschema Design by Form Types", M.Sc. Dissertation, University of Belgrade, Faculty of Electrical Engineering, Department of Informatics, Belgrade, Yugoslavia, June 18, 1993.

[8]   Lukovic I, Mogin P, Pavicevic J, Ristic S, "An Approach to Developing Complex Database Schemas Using Form Types", Software: Practice and Experience, John Wiley & Sons Inc, Hoboken, USA, ISSN: 0038-0644, DOI: 10.1002/spe.820, Vol. 37, No. 15, 2007, pp. 1621-1656.

[9]   Lukovic I, Ristic S, Mogin P, On The Formal Specification of Database Schema Constraints, *1st Serbian-Hungarian Joint Symposium on Intelligent System SISY 2003*, September 19-20, 2003, Subotica, Serbia and Montenegro, Proceedings, pp. 125-136.

[10]   Lukovic I, Ristic S, Mogin P, Pavicevic J, "Database Schema Integration Process – A Methodology and Aspects of Its Applying", Novi Sad Journal of Mathematics (Formerly Review of Research, Faculty of Science, Mathematic Series), Serbia, ISSN: 1450-5444, Vol. 36, No. 1, 2006, pp 115-150.

[11]   "MDA Guide Version 1.0.1", document omg/20030601, OMG, accessible on http://www.omg.org/, 2003.

[12]   Mogin P, Lukovic I, Govedarica M, "Database Design Principles, 2nd Edition, University of Novi Sad, Faculty of Technical Sciences, Novi Sad, Serbia and Montenegro, 2004.

[13]   The Object Management Group, http://www.omg.org/, (August, 2008)

[14]   Pavicevic J, "Development of A CASE Tool for Automated Design and Integration of Database Schemas", M.Sc. Dissertation, University of Montenegro, Faculty of Science, Podgorica, Serbia and Montenegro, 2005.

[15]   Ristic S, "Research of Subschema Consolidation Problem", PhD Thesis, University of Novi Sad, Faculty of Economics, Subotica, Serbia and Montenegro, 2003.

[16]   Stahl T, Völter M, "Model Driven Software Development: Technology, Engineering, Management", John Wiley & Sons, Ltd. 2006.

[17]   Seidewitz E, "What Models Mean", IEEE Software, Vol. 20, No. 5, 2003, pp. 26-32.

GenGMF: Efficient editor development for large meta models using the Graphical Modeling Framework

Enrico Schnepel

b+m Informatik GmbH

Berlin

Germany

e.schnepel@bmiag.de

Abstract

When developing graphical editors using the "Graphical Modeling Framework" (GMF) the required models may become very large depending on the size and structure of the meta model. The complexity contained in the GMF models „Graphical Def Model" and „Mapping Def Model" increases over proportional relative to the meta model and is consequently hard to handle. "GenGMF" is an extension to GMF which offers its own GMF-like domain specific language (DSL) and a model to model transformation for generating both above mentioned models. It uses template-like structures to handle the complexity in a different and more efficient way. This allows the creation of a „GenGMF" model describing the editor while containing up to 80 % less model elements than the generated GMF-models. Additionally there is no need to edit the GMF models manually. The concepts as well as the benefit will be described exemplarily with the "dataflow" editor created for the software development environment "base".

1 Motivation

The "b+m Informatik GmbH Berlin" internally uses the model-driven software development environment "base", which allows the generation of a complete application from a set of previously created models. Some of the model types represent a cyclic graph in the mathematical sense of the word. One of these is the "dataflow" model which in particular is used for defining the user interaction in an application dialogue and the data flow in the background. Other model types are "pageflow", which defines a workflow for the application module by connecting dataflow models with allowed transitions, as well as "domain", which defines the database relevant parts for the application.

"base" uses the Eclipse Modeling Framework (EMF) for defining the meta-model. The tree based editors automatically generated by the EMF are used for editing models. Generally spoken a tree cannot represent the semantic behind a graph with its vertexes and edges. Therefore a tree based editor is not suitable for any of the three model types "dataflow", "pageflow" and "domain". (cf. [5])

In order to improve the development of applications using "base" the initial goal was to develop a graphical editor for the "dataflow" model, which is the most frequently used model type in "base".

2 Problem statement

Figure 1 shows a dataflow model as it is displayed in the tree based editor used in "base". The model contains nodes (dark markers) and connections (dotted markers), which in turn connect the parameters contained in the nodes. Due to the visually separated connections from the nodes in the tree, the model cannot be edited in an intuitive way – instead the textual information has to be read and compared visually with other texts in order to understand the meaning of the model. Therefore it is an essential requirement that the graphical editor should visualize the connections, nodes and parameters properly (cf. [1]).

Figure 1: The tree based "dataflow" editor

3 The Graphical Modeling Framework and its complexity

The Graphical Modeling Framework (GMF) uses four models to describe and after-wards generate a graphical editor. The models "Tooling Def Model", "Graphical Def Model" and "Mapping Def Model" can be created using wizards as shown in figure 2 and are understood as platform independent models (PIM). All platform specific information for the editor is stored in a fourth platform specific model (PSM), the "Diagram Gen Model", which is generated using a transformation out of the first three ones. Some configuration options like model validation need to be set here. The editor could be generated from the "Diagram Gen Model".

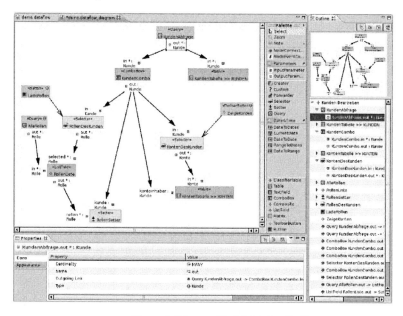

Figure 2: The graphical "dataflow" editor

The wizards know how to create simple nodes and edges with labels in or near by it. They cover only a small subset of the capabilities available in the GMF but it is a good start for beginners to understand the basic principles in GMF. The "Mapping Def Model" - wizard sometimes comes to the wrong assumptions and creates a model containing misleading model references – so the references need to be checked afterwards. Compartments are used to visualize containment structures but the wizards are not capable to handle them at all. Using the Wizard or not – all graphical properties like colors

99

or shapes need to be edited manually in order to change the defaults.

The size of the GMF models increases proportionally with the number of meta model elements in use, making them hard to handle. Most of the GMF model elements contain references to other model elements. When trying to set a reference the GMF often offers all instead of a subset containing only relevant assignment compatible model elements as target for the reference. Additionally adding a new node type to the editor model is frequently done by "copy'n'paste" of an existing part of the model because it is often the easiest way. All this results in a very error-prone handling of the GMF models.

4 Handling complexity with "GenGMF" – a GMF model generator

"base" has a relatively large meta model which defines 20 model element types which can be placed directly under the root element of the "dataflow" model. 18 of them, named "nodes", contain additional child elements, mainly input and output parameters. Nodes are used to describe the processing of data like a parameterized database query or a drop down text field. The parameters are connected using a „NodeConnection" element. Using the GMF for the targeted „dataflow" editor was much too complex due to the amount of element types.

"GenGMF" extends the GMF and provides a model-driven solution to generate the GMF models "Graphical Def Model" (*.gmfgraph) and "Mapping Def Model" (*.gmfmap) as shown in figure 3. It has been designed with large meta models in mind. "GenGMF" defines its own EMF based meta-model and uses a modified EMF tree editor for editing the "GenGMF" models. (cf. [4])

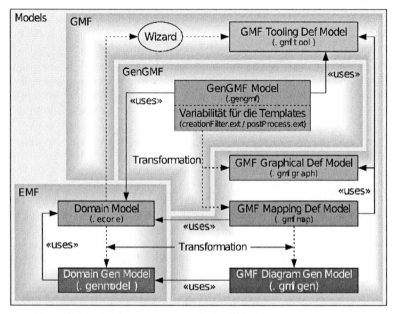

Figure 3: The development process of „GenGMF"

As a basic principle "GenGMF" defines templates and descriptors. A template describes the common basic layout of a group of similar looking figures. They contain model elements "borrowed" from the GMF as defined in the "gmfgraph" meta model. In a „GenGMF" model every basic figure layout is defined only once. In contrast – a descriptor connects a template with an element type from the domain meta-model and a tool element defined in a GMF "Tooling Def Model". During a "GenGMF" specific transformation the templates are copied for every referencing descriptor and are stored into the "Graphical Def Model". The "Mapping Def Model" is automatically created from scratch using the information stored in the descriptors and appropriately set up to reference the corresponding elements in the domain meta-, "Tooling Def"- or "Graphical Def Model".

There are three different types of templates as well as of descriptors. Connections in the diagram are defined using the "EdgeTemplate" / "EdgeDesc" elements. Nodes are defined using the "Node*" or "Compartment*" variants. A Compartment is needed to describe a diagram node containing additional child elements like the attributes in UML Class diagram node.

For some figures in the diagram it might be a requirement to show the name of the meta class in the diagram (e.g. between guillemots "«...»" like in a UML class diagram). To

101

achieve this, a label has to be created containing the text "__CLASSNAME__" which will be replaced during the transformation with the name of the meta class referenced in the descriptor.

Due to the fact that descriptors do not define differences for the figure descriptions of distinct element types a script interface can be used for this purpose. Every model element created during the transformation can modified using scripts. The first script variant "creationFilter" allows to dynamically change the type of a GMF model element during the transformation, e.g. to use a "RoundedRectangle" instead of a "Rectangle" for a particular figure. The second variant "postProcessingFilter" is used to modify the model elements after the transformation but before persisting the model. Using the post processing it is possible to define one template and two figures with different background colors which is shown in listing 1 for the exemplarily used node type "Creator".

```
FigureDescriptor filterCreatorFigureDescriptor(FigureDescriptor fd,
FigureDesc d )
:    fd.actualFigure.setBackgroundColor(192,255,192) // light green
;
```

Listing 1: Setting the background color for a specific node type

Both GMF and "GenGMF" are too complex to fit the logic behind the scenes in a wizard. A wizard (like the one in GMF for the "Graphical Def"- or "Mapping Def Model") to create templates or descriptors in a "GenGMF" model is currently not available and does not seem to be useful. This is because "GenGMF" is intended for large editors where the describing model is more complex than the one for a small editor. The modeler mostly knows how to use the GMF and adopts his knowledge on the very similar template and descriptor structures in "GenGMF".

As mentioned before "GenGMF" has been designed to work with large meta models. The drawback in the handling of GMF models has been mostly eliminated in „GenGMF". In contrast to the GMF nodes or connections – that should look similar in the final editor but are not identical – have to be described only once here.

4.1 The "dataflow" editor

The graphical "dataflow" editor shown in figure 4 has been created by using the "GenGMF" framework. The "GenGMF" model contains three templates (connections, nodes and parameters) and 24 descriptors (20 node, two parameter as well as two for connection types).

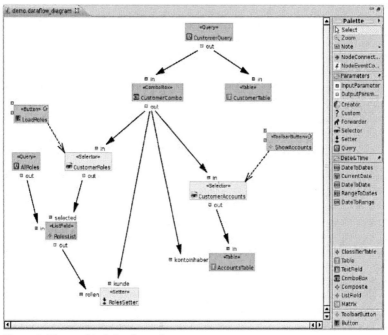

Figure 4: The graphical dataflow editor

The created "GenGMF" model contains 113 elements whereas the generated GMF models "Graphical Def Model" and "Mapping Def Model" contain together 446 elements. Without "GenGMF" it would have been necessary to create the GMF models manually, but now the „GenGMF" model ist 75% smaller than the generated GMF ones thus reducing the effort to create the model(s).

5 Conclusion

"GenGMF" is a model driven solution to generate the GMF models "Graphical Def Model" as well as "Mapping Def Model". It takes much less effort to create a "GenGMF" model and generate the GMF models instead of modifying model skeletons created by the GMF wizards or creating the complete models manually. In the case of the "dataflow" editor this effect was around 75%. Higher rates – depending on the diagram editor to be created – are possible. "GenGMF" has played off its strength – the creation of a graphical editor for a large meta model.

References

[1]   Haller, Steffen Heiko Matthias: Mappingverfahren zur Wissensorganisation, Diplomarbeit, Freie Universität Berlin (2002), URL http://www.knowledgeboard.-com/download/1672/pdf-filename-mapping_wissorg_haller.pdf [24.11.2008]

[2]   Lescot, Jacques et.al.: Bug 206778 – Provide a model oriented Outline View (2008), URL https://bugs.eclipse.org/bugs/show_bug.cgi?id=206778 [25.11.2008]

[3]   Schnepel, Enrico: Entwicklung eines graphischen Editors zur Unterstützung eines modellgetriebenen Softwarenetwicklungsprozesses (2008), Diplomarbeit, Fach-hochschule für Technik und Wirtschaft Berlin, URL http://www.randomice.net/files/Diplomarbeit_Schnepel.pdf [25.11.2008]

[4]   Schnepel, Enrico: GenGMF – a GMF model generator, project website, URL http://gengmf.randomice.net/ [25.11.2008]

[5]   Terfloth, Axel; Wendler, Svenja und Habiger, Marc: Domänenspezifische Edi-toren für die Entwicklung von Embedded Systems (2007), URL http://www.itemis.de/binary.ashx?id=3387 [25.11.2008]

Modelling Behaviour by Activity Diagrams and Complete Code Generation

Erwin Neuhardt

Fachhochschule Schmalkalden

Fakultät Informatik

Blechhammer

D-98574 Schmalkalden

Germany

Abstract

Models play a central role in model driven software development. The code is only secondary and should be generated from models as far as possible. While it is well understood that the static structure of a software system can be described by class diagrams, it is not clear what to use for describing behaviour. UML offers different ways for modelling behaviour. In this paper activity diagrams are used for modelling behaviour. Starting with class diagrams which give the static structure each operation of a class is described by an activity. It is investigated what elements are needed inside the activity to give a complete description of the behaviour. The essential algorithms for code generation are also described. A case study shows how this method can be applied. The case study also shows that the current modelling tools are not very well suited for this kind of modelling. Entering the data often is not very comfortable and not all needed information is shown in activity diagrams.

1 Introduction

Model driven software development puts a strong emphasis on models. They are not only useful artifacts on the way to the code but primary results. UML is mostly used for creating these models. The models are then transformed in several transformation steps into code which a compiler will convert into an executable program [11], p. 11. These transformations are well understood for the static structure of the system and can be done automatically to a large extent. In fact the way from a domain model which describes business contents via a design model describing software classes to classes in an object oriented programming language is not so large. Therefore an automated transformation is not so difficult. The transformation rules from UML classes to Java classes can be found e. g. in [8], Ch. 4.1. But executable software also needs a description of the behaviour. Even in model driven software development, behaviour description is mostly done by adding code manually. There are several possibilities to combine generated and manually created code [11], pp. 159.

105

Describing behaviour in models is a more difficult task and it is a long way from use case descriptions to the implementation of methods in software classes. UML has several diagrams for describing behaviour and at the beginning it is not clear which is the best one to use. In this paper activity diagrams are used for describing behaviour. Activity diagrams have been reworked when UML 2.0 was introduced. They are now able to model behaviour on different levels of abstraction: from more abstract ones as business processes to more concrete ones as operations of a class. This paper investigates how activity diagrams can complement class diagrams in order to model a software system. Class diagrams are used for the static structure, activity diagrams are used for the dynamics of the system. The goal is a complete code generation from the model without any manually added code. We investigate which elements of activity diagrams are needed for the description of behaviour, how they can be used in the models and how the corresponding code can be generated. The programming language Java will be the target language for the code generator.

The rest of the paper is organized al follows: In Section 2, we describe the elements which will be used for modelling the static structure and the behaviour. Section 3 contains the algorithms for code generation and some checks which will guarantee a valid model. A short case study follows in Section 4. Section 5 presents related work.

2 Modelling

This section presents the elements of the static and dynamic model for a software system. We start with class diagrams and discuss the elements for activity diagrams afterwards.

Our modelling is primary suited for the application logic in business information systems. It is characteristic for these systems that objects seldom have states with different behaviour [4], p. 487. Therefore state diagrams do not give much information. Complete code generation needs the static structure as well as the behaviour description. The static structure will be modelled by class diagrams. If the system is simple, the structure can directly be described in a class diagram. According to [4], pp. 302, we assume that there are one or several controller classes which are the starting points for the application logic. If the system is more complex, a decomposition into components is needed. Then, we assume that there are components with interfaces which the components implement [10], Ch. 3.14. In this case, a class diagram shows the classes of a component. In our description we concentrate on those elements of class diagrams which are necessary for complete code generation.

Classes are located in packages, so we first create the package structure. Each class contains attributes and operations. An attribute contains the following information: name and type of the attribute, visibility and static information. An operation contains the following information: name of the operation, visibility, static, parameters, type of the return value and thrown exceptions. Each parameter needs a name and a type. The types of attributes, parameters and return values can be primitive data types as well as other classes. Further associations between classes are needed. Each association has a multiplicity and a role name at both ends. An association can also be directed. Furthermore, classes can specialize other classes and can implement interfaces. Interfaces have the stereotype «interface» and a similar description as classes but no attributes. In order to use already existing classes in the model, e.g. classes from the Java Runtime Environment, classes can have the stereotype «classexisting» and packages can have the stereotype «packageexisting». The stereotype «classexisting» prevents the code generator from generating code for this class, the stereotype «packageexisting» prevents the code generator from generating code for all classes in this package.

There are two types of operations. First, there are operations which are generated by the code generator. The behaviour of these operations is completely determined by the code generator. This is used for constructors and the set/get-operations for attributes. These operations need not be modelled in the class diagram although they can be used in the behaviour description of other operations. Secondly, there are operations which are described by an activity. Each of these operations is assigned an activity which describes the behaviour of the operation. The activity contains a set of actions which are executed in the order determined by the control flow. Two types of actions are used: CallOperationActions and CallBehaviourActions. A CallOperationAction represents a call to another operation. Such an action needs the name of the operation, the name and the class of the object for which the operation is called, the return value und the names and the types of the parameters. A CallBehaviourAction contains one or more statements in the choosen language. These statements are written into the name of the action, because this is the only way to show the statements in activity diagrams in most modelling tools. The choosen language can be Java or any other language which allows the description of primitive behaviour. When Java is choosen, the code generation for these actions only places the contents of the name of the action into the implementation of the operation. When a more abstract language like Action Semantic Language [7] is choosen, the code generator must also translate these actions into the target language, e.g. Java. CallBehaviourActions allow all types of statements including conditional branches, loops, exception handling and calls to other operations. Therefore it is possible to model the behaviour of an operation only as a sequence of CallBehaviourActions or even only as one action, but this would be a poor kind of modelling. Therefore, the following chapters present the modelling for conditions, loops, exception handling and behaviour description distributed to several objects.

A better way of modelling is to describe the control flow by corresponding elements in order to have a graphical representation. Branches with conditions can be described with DecisionNodes and MergeNodes. A DecisionNode has one incoming ActivityEdge and two outgoing ActivityEdges. The outgoing ActivityEdges need a guard which contains a boolean expression or the word "else". A MergeNode contains two incoming ActivityEdges and one outgoing ActivityEdge. To each DecisionNode there is a MergeNode which merges the two branches going out of a DecisionNode. Branches can be nested as long as the nesting is well-formed. This means that the branches of an inner DecisionNode must be merged before branches of the outer DecisionNodes are merged. Fig. 1 shows well-formed and not well-formed activities.

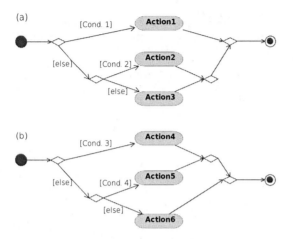

Fig. 1 Well-formed (a) and not well-formed (b) activities

A loop is modelled by a StructuredActivityNode which has the stereotype «loopaction». The name of the node contains the loop condition and a possible initialisation for the loop. The loop body can be modelled with the same elements as activities because they all are allowed inside a StructuredActivityNode. This type of modelling enables pre-checked loops like "for (…) {…}" or "while (…) {..}" but not post-checked loops like "do {…} while (…)". A loop is shown in Fig. 2.

Exceptions can be thrown in CallBehaviourActions with the statement "throw new ExceptionClass()" in the name of the action. In order to catch an exception an ExceptionHandler is needed. Actions like CallOperationActions, CallBehaviourActions and StructuredActivityNodes allow a connection to one or several ExceptionHandlers. The ExceptionHandler has an InputPin which holds the name and the type of the exception. The corresponding exception class must be modelled as a class. When the exception is caught, the actions to be executed are located in the body of the ExceptionHandler. In the case of several ExceptionHandlers exist, the order of the handlers is not shown in the graphical model but it is part of the internal structure. In order to have exception handling for several actions a StructuredActivityNode with stereotype «tryblock» is used. Fig. 2 shows the different types of modelling exception handling.

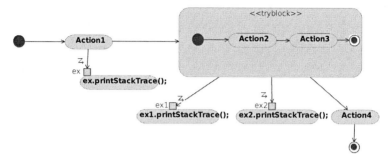

Fig. 2 Modelling of exception handling

The order of execution of the actions is determined by the control flow. Actions like CallBehaviourActions and CallOperationActions as well as StructuredActivityNodes have one incoming and one outgoing ActivityEdge. Every activity has one InitialNode which starts the execution and one ActivityFinalNode where the execution ends. The same conditions hold inside the StructuredActivityNodes.

It is also possible to have several activities in one activity diagram. This is useful when modelling a responsibility which is distributed to several objects. In the main activity, we then have a CallOperationAction and the behaviour of the operation inside the CallOperationAction is described in a further activity. This activity does not have a direct link to the operation. There is a dependency link between the CallOperationAction and the corresponding activity instead of. This kind of modelling allows to display all relevant interaction for a reponsibility in one diagram. Not all UML tools allow several activities in an activity diagram. In this case the additional activities have to be replaced by StructuredActivityNodes. These allow the same kind of modelling as activities do.

Activities also allow parallel execution and modelling of object flow. Both elements are not used. Parallel execution is not used because it is seldom used during the implementation of application logic [10] Ch. 6.1.4. There are three reasons why object flow is not modelled. First, it is very time consuming to add an object node or a pin to an action. In most UML tools, it takes several mouse clicks and adding text in several dialogs. Secondly, object flow can make the workflow more difficult to understand, even in simple examples. This is shown in an example in Fig. 3. Thirdly, object flow can also include control flow. Then, it is more difficult to determine the order of execution in this case. This situation would improve when a textual editor is imbedded in the modelling tool as described in [9]. Then, text could be edited instead of modelling pins or object nodes and the object flow could be computed automatically. This computation is simple in case of CallOperationActions because all information is structured in attributes of the action but more complex in case of CallBehaviourActions where text has to be analysed.

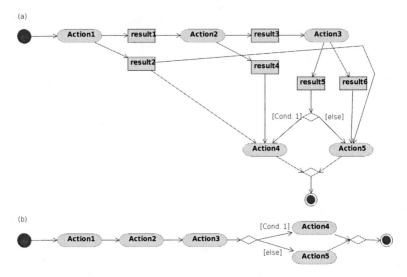

Fig. 3 Same activity with (a) and without (b) object flow

3 Code generation

This section presents the basic algorithms used in the code generator.

The code generator transforms the model into Java classes. It maps packages to Java packages, interfaces to Java interfaces and classes to public Java classes. Attributes which have a primitive data type are mapped to built-in data types in Java. For these attributes a set-method and a get-method is generated. The mapping of attributes with other classes as type and associations depends on the multiplicity. If the multiplicity is less than or equal to one, an object reference is generated as well as set- and get-methods. If the multiplicity is greater than one an object reference to a list is generated. This reference is initialized with an empty ArrayList. Access methods are not generated because the names of these methods do not always follow a naming convention. An ArrayList is not always the best choice, but it works for many cases. For each operation a method in the corresponding Java class is generated. The signature of the operation is taken from the class diagram, the implementation is generated from the assigned activity. This can either be a direct assigned activity or an activity connected with a CallOperationAction.

The transformation of an activity is as follows: Starting at the InitialNode, all actions will be transformed into corresponding pieces of Java code. The order of the code pieces is determined by the control flow. The transformation of an action depends on its type. If the node is a CallBehaviourAction, the name of the node will be taken as piece of code. If the node is a CallOperationAction, a method call is generated. Both types of nodes are embedded in a try-block is the case of existing ExceptionHandlers. The same happens to a StructuredActivityNode with stereotype «tryblock». For each modelled ExceptionHandler a catch-block is generated. A StructuredActivityNode with stereotype «loopaction» is mapped to a loop. The loop condition is taken from the name and all actions inside the StructuredActivityNode are transformed into pieces of code.

The transformation of DecisionNodes and MergeNodes is more complex. First the control flow of the branch with guard not equal to "else" is followed until the next MergeNode is reached. Then the branch with guard "else" is followed until the MergeNode is reached. After that the next node after the MergeNode is followed. This algorithm also works for nested decisions when a nesting level controls the order of execution. The branch with the guard not equal to "else" has always nesting level 0. The "else" branch adds 1 to the current nesting level at the DecisionNode. When a MergeNode is reached, 1 is substracted from the nesting level and then only continued when the nesting level is greater than or equal to 0.

The implementation of an operation ends when the ActivityFinalNode is reached.

An activity must stick to some rules in order to the code generator working correctly. These rules are checked before the code generator is started. First, only the elements described in Section 2 are allowed. Each activity and each StructuredActivityNode has only one InitialNode and only one ActivityFinalNode. This rule excludes the InitialNodes and ActivityFinalNodes in embedded StructuredActivityNodes. The test for valid nesting of DecisionNodes and MergeNodes is more complex. It is done by a successive simplification of the activity or the StructuredActivityNode resp. First, all actions are removed. Then a DecisionNode and its corresponding MergeNode are removed when the MergeNode is the successor of the DecisionNode. This is done as long as possible. The control flow is adopted in each transformation step. The algorithm stops when no more DecisionNodes can be removed. The original acitivity or StructuredActivityNode is valid when the InitialNode is now followed by the ActivityFinalNode.

In order to make modelling easier, the import statement for classes used from other packages is generated. For this purpose, a list of all class names in the model is generated. The elements of this list are checked with the code parts of all activities assigned to an operation of the class under investigation. Only those code parts are considered which precede with a blank character, a "<" character or a "=" character. An import-statement is generated for all elements fulfilling these conditions. The elements are stored in a list in order to avoid double import-statements. This technique still allows to use fully qualified class names in actions.

4 Case Study

A small case study was made in order to evaluate the results. The case study was carried through using MagicDraw 11.6 Community Edition [5] and openArchitectureWare 4.2 [6] which is a plug-in of Eclipse 3.3. MagicDraw only allows one activity per activity diagram. Therefore all additional activities in the diagram must be modelled as StructuredActivityNodes.

The case study contains three classes with associations. Some operations for these classes were also modelled. The example shows a simple examination registration with the classes Registration, Student and Exam. An object of class Student knows all examinations for which the student registered, an object of class Exam knows all students who registered for the examination. The registration object knows all students and all examinations. Additionally there is the class String which is located in the corresponding package.

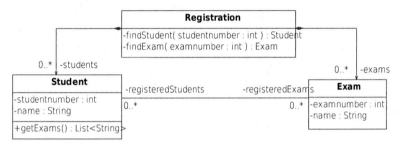

Fig. 4 Class diagram for Registration example

The operation getExamsPerStudent returns the names of all examinations for which a student has registered. The following figure shows the activity for this operation and the operation getExams which is called from getExamsPerStudent.

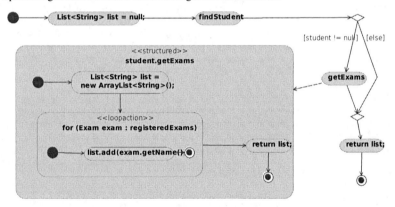

Fig. 5 Activity diagram for operation getExamsPerStudent

Fig. 5 shows that the representation of CallOperationActions does not give enough information. It is not clear where the value of the variable student used in successing actions is set. Actually this happens in findStudent which is a CallOperationAction. A representation as an CallBehaviourAction with name "Student student = findStudent(student_number);" would show this more clearly. On the other hand, CallOperationActions are needed because this is the only way to connect an activity (or StructuredActivityN-ode) with an operation inside an activity diagram.

The model is exported from MagicDraw in an EMF-file. This file is read from openAr-chitectureWare and three Java files are created. The code generator is written in the template language Xpand. Listing 1 shows the processing of ActivityNodes. For each node type there is a special processing and the processing of the following node is called afterwards unless the final node is reached.

```
«DEFINE ActivityNode(Integer level) FOR ActivityNode»
    «IF CallOperationAction.isInstance(this)»
    ...
    «ELSEIF DecisionNode.isInstance(this)»
        «EXPAND DecisionNode(level) FOR this»
    «ELSEIF InitialNode.isInstance(this)»
    ...
    «ELSEIF StructuredActivityNode.isInstance(this)»
        «IF this.getAppliedStereotypes().name.
            contains("loopaction")»
            «EXPAND LoopAction FOR this»
        «ELSEIF this.getAppliedStereotypes().name.
            contains("tryblock")»
            «EXPAND TryBlock FOR this»
        «ENDIF»
        «EXPAND ActivityNode(level) FOR
            this.outgoing.first().target»
    «ELSEIF Action.isInstance(this)»
    ...
    «ENDIF»
«ENDDEFINE»


«DEFINE DecisionNode(Integer level) FOR DecisionNode»
    «IF this.outgoing.size == 2»
        if («getIfCase().guard.body.first()») {
            «EXPAND ActivityNode(0) FOR getIfCase().target»
        }
        else {
            «EXPAND ActivityNode(level+1) FOR
                getElseCase().target»
    «ELSE»
        «LET level-1 AS level»
            «IF level >= 0»
                }
                «EXPAND ActivityNode(level) FOR
                    this.outgoing.first().target»
            «ENDIF»
```

```
«ENDLET»
«ENDIF»
«ENDDEFINE»
```

Listing 1 Processing of ActivityNode and DecisionNode

The language Check is used for writing checks on activities. The transformation for checking well-formed activities is done with Xtend. Listing 2 shows a part of the transformation for checking well-formed activities: Starting with the model, all actions are removed in a recursive call and the control flow is adjusted.

```
Model main (Model model):
    removeAction(model,model.getActiveActions().size )->
    removeDecision(model);
Model removeAction(Model model, Integer count ):
    count <= 0 ? model :
    (removeFirstAction(model) ->
    removeAction(model, count - 1));
Model removeFirstAction(Model model):
    let ac = model.getFirstActiveAction():
    let inflow = ac.incoming.first():
    let outflow = ac.outgoing.first():
    let acNext = ac.outgoing.first().target:
    inflow.setTarget(outflow.target) ->
    (acNext.incoming.size == 1 ?
        acNext.setIncoming({inflow}) :
        acNext.changeInflow(inflow, outflow) )->
    outflow.destroy() ->
    ac.destroy()->
    model;
```

Listing 2 Part of transformation for checking well-formed activities

The Community Edition of MagicDraw only allows 25 actions in a project. Therefore a complete modelling even of this small example needs be distributed among several projets. These projects can be used together in openArchitectureWare by using global variables.

The case study shows that UML tools give little support for this kind of modelling. First, not all information needed is shown. Secondly, the graphical editors lack support for topics like code completion. Special editors are needed in that case. In [9], it is shown how this can be realized.

5 Related work

The tool FUJABA [3] is a joint work of the universities of Paderborn, Kassel, Siegen and Darmstadt. Similar to our approach, it uses class diagrams for the static structure and activity diagrams for behaviour modelling. A complete code generation is possible. There are StatementActions for Java statements, DecisionNodes for conditional branches. Several activities in a diagram are not possible. There are story actions for describing the interaction between objects. On a lower level there are again Java statements in the story actions. Story actions are not part of the UML.

In [2], a transformation from activities to TAAL which is a Java-like programming language is described. The modelling of the activities is similar with the exception of loops. The goal is not creating executable code instead of showing that the transformation from activities to TAAL does not change the semantics.

The tool AndroMDA [1] uses activity diagrams in the cartridge BPM4Struts for modelling the user interface. It generates code for a Web application with the Struts framework. There are actions for creating views and controllers, conditional branching is also possible. Other elements are not used.

The goal of Executable UML [7] is the complete code generation from the model. It uses state diagrams and the Action Semantic Language (ASL) for describing behaviour. ASL is a textual language. Every behaviour which is not represented in states is expressed in textual form.

6 Conclusion

This paper presented a method for describing software systems with class diagrams and activity diagrams for complete code generation. The static structure is modelled in class diagrams whereas activity diagrams give a description of the implementation of the operations. This method allows to model a large part of the application logic of a software system. A code generator generates Java code from the model and integrated checks guarantee that the rules for modelling activities are preserved. The application of the method shows that the current UML tools are not very well suited for that kind of modelling because they do not show enough information in activity diagrams and graphical modelling is sometimes cumbersome. A textual modelling with automatic conversion to a graphical representation would be better in some cases.

References

[1] AndroMDA BPM4Struts Cartridge v.3.2, 09 November 2006, http://www.andromda.org/

[2] Engels G., Kleppe A., Rensink A., Semenyak M., Soltenborn C., Wehrheim H.: From UML Activities to TAAL – Towards Behaviour-Preserving Model Transformations, In: Schieferdecker I., Hartman A. (eds.): ECMDA-FA 2008, LNCS 5095, pp. 94-109, Springer, Heidelberg (2008)

[3] FUJABA Dokumentation v.0.1, 20 March 2002, http://www.fujaba.de/

[4] Larman C.: Applying UML and Patterns, Pearson Education, New York (2005)

[5] MagicDraw , http://www.magicdraw.com/

[6] openArchitectureWare User GuideVersion 4.2, 15 September 2007, http://www.openarchitectureware.org/

[7] Raistrick C., Francis P., Wright J., Carter C., Wilkie I.: Model Driven Architecture with Exceutable UML, Cambridge University Press, Cambridge (2004)

[8] Rumpe B.: Agile Modellierung mit UML, Springer, Heidelberg (2005)

[9] Scheidgen M.: Textual Modelling Embedded into Graphical Modelling, In: Schieferdecker I., Hartman A. (eds.): ECMDA-FA 2008, LNCS 5095, pp. 153-168, Springer, Heidelberg (2008)

[10] Siedersleben J.: Moderne Softwarearchitektur, dpunkt.verlag, Heidelberg (2004)

[11] Stahl Th., Völter M., Efftinge S., Haase A.: Modellgetriebene Softwareentwicklung, dpunkt.verlag, Heidelberg (2007)

[12] Unified Modeling Language: Superstructure, version 2.1.1, 03 February 2007 http://www.uml.org/

Model-Driven Architecture for an Interactive Ajax Mapping Platform

Tobias Weidemann
WSI/GRIS University of Tübingen
Germany
weideman@informatik.uni-tuebingen.de

Tobias Hüttner
MagicMaps, Pliezhausen
Germany
tobias.huettner@magicmaps.de

PD Dr. Frank Hanisch (*)
WSI/GRIS University of Tübingen
Germany
(*) Contact: Frank Hanisch, WSI/GRIS, Sand 14, 72072 Tübingen, Germany

Abstract

We present the model-driven development of highly interactive processes for a Web 2.0 bicycle tracks portal. Using standard UML activity diagrams and extended UML profiles we were able to model the graphical creation and direct manipulation of tracks and the associated server-side and client-side processes. Our abstract model can be transformed into a specific platform model, like e.g. PHP server-side and JavaScript client-side. We demonstrate how existing Ajax frameworks can be embedded in the transformation process and how the transformation can directly generate framework-specific code, here code for the widespread prototype [Proto05] framework.

1 Introduction

Modern Web applications show a tight, dynamic communication between the client and server system. Hidden background processes aim at creating an interaction style similar to the classic Desktop interaction; moreover the user community is now seen as part of system processes, including system and data development. This paradigm is circumscribed as Web 2.0 or Rich Internet Application (RIA). It leads to fundamental changes in the development models of today's companies and requires new methods for software development and interaction design that allow for creating Web applications quickly, modify and extend them flexible, and run them secure.

This contribution presents the mapping portal „ADFC Tourenportal" (http://www.adfc-tourenportal.de), a cooperation between the German bicycle club ADFC (Allgemeiner

117

Deutscher Fahrrad Club) and the company MagicMaps, which has specialized in visualizing interactive 3D maps. It is a good example and test object, because the project contains not only traditional Web portal processes like as user management, session control, content selection and download, but also the highly interactive and complex processes required for creating and manipulating a network of bicycle tracks. Tasks like these are normally performed by a geographic information system (GIS); however in the given project they had to become part of a Web-based authoring system.

Given that Web 2.0 code usually is hard to maintain or even to evolve, we have introduced a model-driven software development process. We could demonstrate in this project that model-driven software engineering can be applied to Ajax-driven Web 2.0 software and that it can leverage development using standard process modeling and rapid prototyping of the graphical user interface.

We use standards like the Unified Modeling Language (UML) and the activity diagrams defined herein and extend these by using the UML extension mechanisms (profile, tagged values, etc.); a specialized UML profile is defined that can be used to model the server and the client-side of the interaction process. This model can then be transformed into a platform specific model, e.g. PHP on server side or JavaScript on client side. Especially interesting is the fact that existing Ajax frameworks can be embedded in the transformation process and the transformation can directly generate artefacts on the basis of such a framework. We show this in our project with the well-known Ajax JavaScript framework prototype [Proto05].

The remainder of this text is structured as follows. Chapter 2 provides an overview of the model-driven architecture pattern, Ajax design patterns, and Web mapping services. The concrete project setting is described in Chapter 3, together with a specification of the desired software solution – explanative in form of use cases. Chapter 4 details our approach to activity modeling and Ajax transformations for two central Ajax patterns. Results are shown and discussed in Chapter 5.

2 Related Work

2.1 The Model Driven Architecture Pattern

In 2000 the Object Management Group (OMG), a computer industry consortium that created the UML and related industry standards, drafted the Model Driven Architecture (MDA) [Soley00]. This soon to be finished architecture [OMG03, OMG05] provides a forward-oriented, model-driven software development process that strictly separates functionality and technology. Of special interest with respect to Web applications like ours is that most software code can be automatically generated from abstract models, thereby enhancing the reusability of models as well as the maintenance and evolution of the code.

The process is a typical model transformation in model-driven software development, placing emphasis on the automatic transformation of one model into another. The MDA pattern identifies three distinct models (see Figure 1): the Computation Independent Model (CIM), the Platform Independent Model (PIM), and the Platform Specific Model

(PSM). The CIM models requirements of the system and may not inherit information whether parts are computation-oriented or not [OMG03]. It is meant as business model that communicates underlying processes to architects and developers of the software solution. A CIM may cover different views on the system – even in several models. The technical system is described in a PIM; however it does not contain any platform-specific information. The PSM finally combines the given information of a PIM with information about how it interacts with and uses a specific platform. It contains all information necessary to generate the final code. The OMG explicitly states the possibility to consider the generated code itself a PSM.

Note that the OMG does not define any details of the shown transformations. Only their source and target (for example PIM and PSM) are specified, the actual transformation is undefined. This could be the transformation scheme.

A natural transition from a code-oriented view to a model-oriented one in software development is shown in [Bézivin01]. The authors point out similarities between OMGs meta object facility (as described in [MOF03]) and grammars for programming languages. According to them the crucial step in the perception of software development was when creating and working with models became part of the production process; therefore means of model serialization have to be provided. They present an exemplary architecture in which aspects of technology and functionality are strictly separated and lead, by characterizing implementations in middleware tools, to the description of the automatic transformation of models.

[Melia05] present a standardized specification of visual and textual elements in such transformations. Their approach expresses a two-stage transformation process in QVT-P (Query/Views/Transformation, [QVTP03]) notation. After modeling the systems' functional aspects in a "navigation model" and architectonic aspects in a "configuration model", they combine these representations into a first transformation, an "integration model" that is still platform-independent. This model is then transformed by a second transformation into one or several platform-specific models.

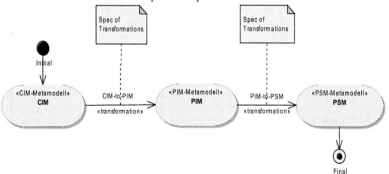

Figure 1: The Model Driven Architecture pattern identifies three distinct models, the Computation Independent Model (CIM), the Platform Independent Model (PIM), and the Platform Specific Model (PSM).

2.2 Ajax Patterns

Web 2.0 concepts typically describe a user-centered, dynamic network as opposed to the rather author-centered, static Web 1.0. [OReilly05] named these key principles: scalable Web services that can be extended and redesigned with a growing number of users, rich data sources that are co-developed by users and thereby make use of the wisdom of the crowd, customer self-service not restricted to a single device, and lightweight programming models that allow for rich user interfaces and coupling with other systems.

"Rich" user interfaces refers mainly to the use of Ajax (Asynchronous JavaScript and XML) technology over interactive Java/Flash components, demonstrated for example in Google Gmail or Yahoo Flickr. Technically, Ajax uses the Document Object Model and XmlHttpRequest for dynamic data interchange and manipulation and asynchronous data retrieval. It makes heavy use of JavaScript to binding everything together and to allow for direct manipulation, the latter often by offering drag and drop. JavaScript development is laborious due to missing high-level structures and browser incompatibilities; the lack of modularity renders project management ineffective and tedious [Hanson07]. This is another, more technical reason to prefer modeling over low-level programming for Ajax applications.

The Google Web Toolkit toolkit [Hanson07] represents a first step by letting programmers write client-side Java code and translating it to JavaScript; instead of trying to enhance the Ajax core, they transfer programming to an object-oriented language and take advantage of already available tools, like e.g. an integrated developing environment with support for markup, debugging and versioning. However they focus on interface programming instead of process modeling.

Emerging Ajax design patterns can be found for example in [Mahemoff06]. Of interest here are Predictive Fetch, Multi-Stage Download, Suggestion, and Microlink. Predictive Fetch loads data under the assumption that it is needed soon, although the data is irrelevant in the current state. The Multi-Stage Download pattern describes the incremental page assembly that loads the basic, static page structure first, and then dynamically the other content components. It reduces network delays and preserves control over display order. The Suggestion pattern represents an input field with a list of elements that are likely to match the user's next input. The list is updated dynamically using XmlHttpRequest, and may use server-side matching tests with complexity ranging from simple String comparison to semantic tests using e.g. knowledge from previous user interactions. Suggestion increases usability by avoiding typing errors and offering possibly unknown alternatives, and can further enhance application efficiency by reducing the amount of user interactions required for navigation and completing a task. The Microlink pattern finally describes a link that expands a small page area; it is usually used for context information and graphical annotations. Microlink avoids the user distraction and interaction slowdown that are otherwise caused by a full page reload.

2.3 Web Mapping and Tracks

Web mapping services, as opposed to GIS services, focus on visualization and direct user navigation. While mapping-related Web services had been available already from geographic information system (GIS) vendors such as the Environmental Systems Research Institute (ESRI), AOL MapQuest, or Microsoft MapPoint, it was the Ajax-based Google Maps that brought the idea to the masses, providing a simple graphical user interface with other Web 2.0 paradigms [OReilly05]. Google Maps, a free web mapping service with street maps and satellite images, offers data enrichment through user-side annotations, mainly to classify and find places of interest. Users can further define start and end point of a route; the server tries then provides driving directions for cars, mass transit directions, and walking directions for pedestrians. The route can be directly manipulated by inserting user-defined checkpoints, however it cannot be saved.

Besides Google Maps, only few vendors offer walking directions, like e.g. MapQuest or Ask.com. Instead, routing services typically focus on driving directions for cars, for which they often integrate up-to-date traffic information; however in all instances, bikers are left out. The Google Maps 'Bike There" feature request petition [Smith07] therefore aims to get bicycle directions for Google Maps with more than 40.000 total signatures as of August 2008. They point out that the difference from a simple "avoid highways" checkbox is that bikers favor low-traffic streets, prefer bike lanes, fat shoulders, and might need help finding a way around steep hills.

None of these providers offers a touring service enabling users to view tracks. This gap is currently filled with touring platforms, communities that collect track information for local areas. These local platforms are not interconnected, and currently not integrated into one of the widespread web mapping services.

The online platform GPSies [GPSies06] started in 2006. Here users can upload their own GPS tracks or create tracks by drawing them based on a displayed map-background. Tracks are not restricted to biking, but can also be filed in categories such as "horse riding", "hiking" or "motorcycling". However, dynamically routing within a given network is rendered impossible because single tracks are not interconnected. In contrast to other comparable services the content is created not by editors but the users themselves.

The Geo Coaching [Pröbstl04] research project was developed in 2004 at the University of Natural Resources and Applied Life Sciences in Vienna to evaluate GPS technology in leisure and recreation. The intention was to collect and aggregate GPS data on which further research can be based on this platform. In the meantime the portal is further developed independently as a spin-off. The available tracks are examined and cannot be changed by the users. They are available in various formats for importing them into PDA software or GPS devices. The tracks are filed in categories such as "biking", "nordic walking" or "horse riding".

3 Project Goals

The project was initiated to improve and modify the software architecture of an already existing Web-based GPS track solution for the German bicycle club ADFC. This portal allows the users to find, buy, and rate GPS-based tracks. Project goals were to develop Ajax-based components that provide a highly interactive routing and that improve the given community support. The method of choice was model-driven user interface development, with which the following use cases had to be modified.

121

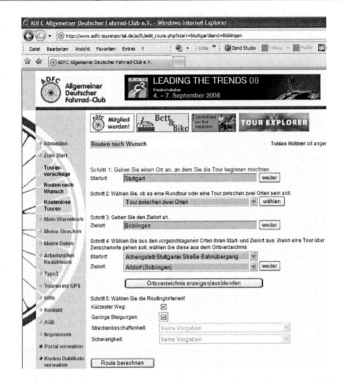

Figure 2: This user interface of the routing algorithm had to be evolved.

Use Case 1: Generation of an individual track by the user with a routing algorithm.

At the beginning of our project the process of generating individual tracks was synchronous only and without interactivity. The user had to enter all necessary information in advance, and then he could issue the routing request; after getting the routing result after some waiting time he had to start over again with the same process (see Figure 2). The user had many severe drawbacks with this synchronous approach. During the waiting time the application blocked and the user could not do anything useful in the meantime (e.g. browsing the map). Furthermore, the alteration of routing conditions was tedious and error prone since the user had to start the complete parameter input process over and over again. Figure 3 shows, on the other hand, a calculated route in the new interface.

Use Case 2: Process of track combination.

At the beginning of our project the respective tracks were added manually, and higher level track hierarchies were generated. They are called "course" on the first level and "tour" on the second hierarchy level. The aggregation was done manually by adding unique identifiers of tracks or courses into the newly generated hierarchy element. This hierarchy element doesn't contain geometry like an ordinary track but holds a list of identifiers referencing to objects of the hierarchy level below (see Figure 4).

This process had to be modified so that the single tracks or courses are no longer selected manually by putting identifiers into hierarchy elements but are selected automatically by using the improved routing algorithm (see Use Case 1) to generate the list of identifiers of the hierarchy element by routing.

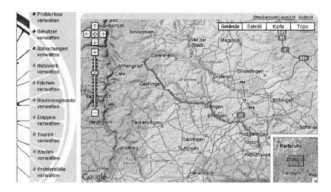

Figure 3: This highly interactive routing interface resulted from applying our model-driven development approach. The user can recalculate a route by repositioning the end flags.

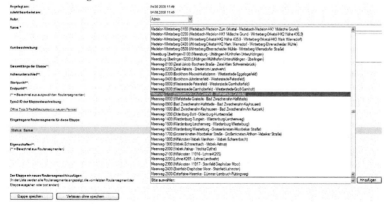

Figure 4: At the beginning of our project, tracks had to be selected manually by putting identifiers into hierarchy elements.

3.1 Activity Modeling and Ajax Transformations

Our developed approach can generate source code for Ajax-driven Web applications automatically from given architecture models. It involves creating an initial model of the system, transforming it into another model out of which source code is finally generated. Our approach uses a transformation process according to the MDA pattern and thus defines a two-stage process for modeling and code-generation.

In a first step we modeled the interaction flow with an activity diagram, a presentational form that we have chosen due to the high level of interactivity of our Ajax-driven Web application. All modeling tasks were made with Enterprise Architect 7.0 by Sparx Systems that offers graphical modeling of software in UML – model types according to version 2.1.1 of the UML specification are supported.

Single activities are annotated with stereotypes and tagged values that represent the semantics of the desired Ajax functionality. Annotations of model elements and connectors can be realized in UML with stereotypes and tagged values. Stereotypes are extensions to model elements in a specific context. In a given example an element "webapplication xy" could be annotated with the stereotype <<project>>. So called "tagged values" are property-definitions in UML. In this example meaningful tagged values to "webapplication xy" with the stereotype <<project>> would be "project manager=[name of project manager]" or "budget=[height of budget]".

These annotations control the transformation templates, which transform the activity diagram into a class diagram. The class diagram is then transformed into code. It inherits all objects and the connectors between them, and is again annotated with stereotypes and tagged values that control code generation. The modeled activity diagram contains both the information about the technical system and about the user interaction flow, so it can be considered a PIM in the sense of the MDA pattern. A specific set of annotations has been defined and tested. It can be extended to include more sophisticated transformations.

One simple example of an Ajax-based application is an interface enabling a user to search for cities. Figure 5 shows the modeled interaction flow in form of an activity diagram which has been annotated with stereotypes and tagged values. This activity diagram is now to be transformed into a class diagram. This class diagram inherits all objects and the connectors between them, again annotated by stereotypes and tagged values which control code generation. The second step comprises the code generation based on this class diagram. Figure 6 shows the class diagram that was generated from of the activity diagram shown in Figure 5.

The transformations are carried out again with Enterprise Architect functionality. Besides generating models for the purpose of documentation, the software also offers the possibility to transform diagrams of a certain type into diagrams of another type by model transformations in form of "MDA transformations". These transformations are individual transformations that transform fragments of diagrams from one domain into another. Each transformation is controlled by the corresponding template. The template defines how attributes and connectors to other elements are mapped into the target domain. Model-to-model transformations are called "transformation templates", whereas model-to-code transformations are called "code generation templates". The syntax of both is defined in a simple language called "code generation template language". Templates for platform-specific transformations and code generation in the languages C, C++, C#, Delphi, Java, PHP, Python, ActionScript, Visual Basic and VB.NET are provided, however not for Ajax/JavaScript. We therefore had to develop templates for the first transformation (activity diagram to class diagram) and code generation templates for our purpose. Since our Web application is based on PHP (server-side) and JavaScript (client-side), and Enterprise Architect already ships with code generation templates for PHP, we only had to develop code generation templates for client side JavaScript code.

They covered transforming a PIM into a PSM considering specific Ajax behavior. The developed code generation templates covered transforming into JavaScript code with respect to framework-specific XmlHttpRequests.

The transformation for the Ajax patterns XmlHttpRequest works as follows. All browsers with JavaScript functionality offer XmlHttpRequest to trigger a server request, usually to alter and present information dynamically. As such, XmlHttpRequest can be seen as basic communication pattern. Although semantics vary, the basic principle is more or less the same: The controlling JavaScript instantiates an XmlHttpRequest object with information about the target host and with communication parameters, and initiates the request. This can be done asynchronously to avoid blocking the browser until a response is transmitted. As soon as a response is received, it is typically processed by triggering registered event listeners or callback functions. We modeled a XmlHttpRequest first by assigning stereotypes to the flows representing request and response (called "xmlHtttpRequest" and "xmlHttpResponse") and second by assigning tagged values to annotate the flow with the communication domain ("domain=communication") and the request flow with the type of communication ("communicationType=XmlHttpRequest").

The Ajax Suggestion pattern has been chosen for a new design of the user mask that allows editing a bike route network - the user should be enabled to directly navigate to a city or a bike route by typing the beginning letters of the name. While typing, we dynamically transmit a server request and present its answer to the user (see Figure 7), making it selectable for the user. We modeled the Suggestion pattern by annotating different actions and flows with stereotypes and tagged values. The server request and response were annotated as before. Script and browser actions such as "showInterface" or "queryCities" were annotated to belong to the client domain (tagged value "domain=client"), whereas the user input of a city name was modeled by a so-called "interaction-flow" (by being stereotype "interaction"). Reacting on user input on character base was modeled by a decision element (tagged values "domain=client" and "task=handleInteraction"). Initiation of the XmlHttpRequest process is modeled by a so called "controlFlow" (stereotype "controlFlow").

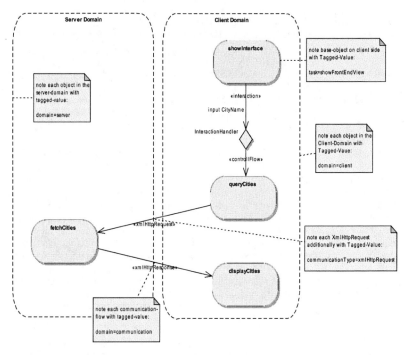

Figure 5: Activity diagram modeling the interaction flow – annotated with stereotypes and tagged values.

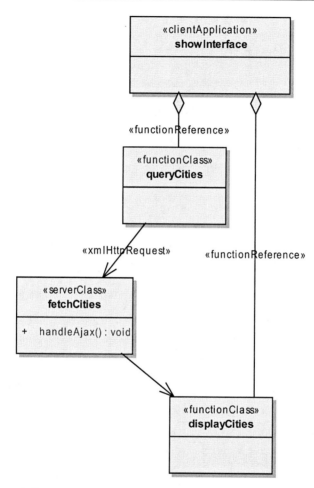

Figure 6: Class diagram generated from of the activity diagram in Figure 5.

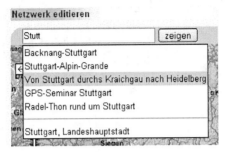

Figure 7: Our realization of the Suggestion pattern for bike routes.

4 Results

The central component is the interactive track generation via routing and the user directly interacting with the map on a single interface. This process is no longer organized synchronously (first input, the result, then maybe input again, see Use Case 1) but asynchronously by the application of Web 2.0 concepts – input and result are woven together, the input parameters can be directly seen in the map where also the result is shown. The generation of higher order track hierarchies based on existing tracks is now possible interactively and direct manipulative; the hierarchy levels are generated by routing and no longer by manual selection (see Use Case 2).

At the beginning of our project the process for editing the geometry of the bike tracks entailed, as a first step, the exporting of the existing track points into an external file. This file had to be edited externally before it could be uploaded to the portal. In a second step this newly given segment was annotated with metadata (e.g. track type). The third step involved combining several of these segments to one course – by assigning a segment to the course and then deciding if the course is complete; if not, another segment could be added and so on. Metadata could also be entered for this course. The fourth and last step in this process was to combine several courses into one tour, a subprocess that corresponds to the previous step: one course at a time could be added to the tour and finally metadata had to be entered. A model of this process is given in Figure 8.

We reworked this tedious process of editing geometry and hierarchical information of the network into a nonlinear mode. Using a map interface the user can now directly and graphically manipulate tours. Routing algorithms take over the task of selecting several adjoining segments. The entire development process was model-driven. Figure 9 shows the new interactive process of editing network geometry and hierarchy.

Our framework shares the advantages of other model-driven architectures [OMG03].

- A valuable result from our approach is that existing models can now be fitted easily to a new target RIA infrastructure (for example to Microsoft Silverlight or Adobe Air), since it does not contain platform-specific prerequisites in modeling step, here the activity diagram. Different interaction and communication types can be integrated by extending the set of used stereotypes and tagged values and creating transformation templates for these. Because code generation is handled in the usual MDA manner by creating source code out of a class diagram, different target languages are supported by using the appropriate templates.

- It helps in integration as the available activity diagram shows communication-intensive activities and thus enables planning and adjusting necessary system components.
- It helps in maintenance as automated load and performance testing can be based on certain stereotypes and tagged values. User interactions or communication flows with characteristic high-bandwidth communication can be marked as such and specialized test cases can consider this behavior.
- It can be used to validate the system against requirements as transformation templates transfer the diagrams into each other in a known way. Based on these templates validation routines can be created which look at the code and the models in inverse direction.

None of these characteristics were available before we reworked the system.

5 Conclusion

We have experienced in our project that a model-driven approach can leverage the development of highly interactive processes for rich internet applications, here for a Web 2.0 bicycle tracks portal. Basically we have adopted the MDA pattern and model user interactions with standard activity diagrams.

Future work will consider refinements of the defined annotation set as well as the transformation templates. Extending them will enable us to model more sophisticated user interfaces and hopefully help to lower barriers for architects of modern Web applications when considering a model-driven approach.

References

[Bézivin01] J. Bézivin (2001), From Object Composition to Model Transformation with the MDA. In: Proceedings of TOOLS'USA, vol. IEEE TOOLS-39, pp. 346-354.

[GPSies06] K. Bechtold (2006), GPSies – Tracks for Vagabonds, Berlin, Germany. http://www.gpsies.com

[Hanson07] R. Hanson and A. Tacy (2007), GWT in Action, Easy Ajax with the Google Web Toolkit.

[Mahemoff06] M. Mahemoff (2006), Ajax Design Patterns. O'Reilly Media Inc., Sebastopol, USA.

[Melia05] S. Melia, A. Kraus, N. Koch (2005), MDA Transformations Applied to Web Application Development, University of Alicante, Spain.

[MOF03] Object Management Group (OMG) (2003), Meta Object Facility Core Specification (MOF) Version 2.0. Adopted Specification, ptc/03-10-04, Oct. 2003.

[OMG03] Object Management Group (OMG) (2003), MDA GuideVersion 1.0.1, omg/2003-06-01

[OMG05] Object Management Group (OMG) (2005), UML 2.1.1 – Unified Modeling Language (UML) Superstructure. Version 2.1.1. Final Adopted Specification, formal/07-02-05.

[OReilly05] T. O'Reilly (2005), What is Web 2.0, Design Patterns and Business Models for the Next Generation of Software, O'Reilly Network. http://www.oreillynet.com/pub/a/oreilly/tim/news/2005/09/30/what-is-web-20.html

[Pröbstl04] U. Pröbstl, L. Lampl. (2004), Geo-coaching – neue Entwicklungen für Freizeit und Tourismus in der Landschaft. In Strobl, J., Blaschke, T., Griesebner, G. (Hrsg.): AGIT Spezial 2004: eTourismus und Geoinformatik – Interdisziplinäre Fachtagung Salzburg.

[Proto05] Prototype Javascript Framework (2005). http://www.prototypejs.org

[QVTP03] QVT Partners (2003), Initial Submission for MOF 2.0 Query/ View/ Transformations RFP, QVT-Partners.

[Smith07] P. Smith (2007), Google Maps 'Bike There'. http://googlemapsbikethere.org

[Soley00] R. Soley and the OMG Staff Strategy Group, Object Management Group (2000), Model Driven Architecture, White Paper, Draft 3.

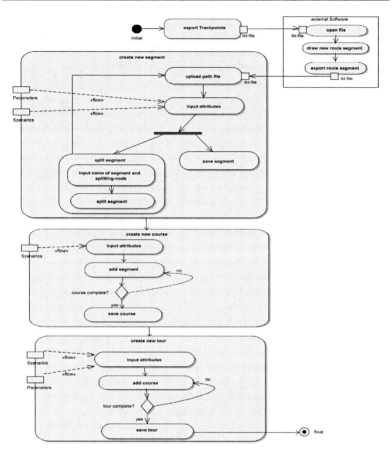

Figure 8: A model of the previous process of editing network hierarchies.

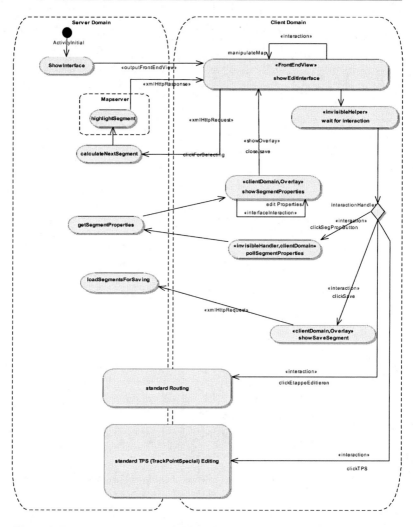

Figure 9: The reworked process of editing network hierarchies (simplified for clarity).

Customizing the JET2 Template Engine

Marc-Florian Wendland
Zeppelinstraße 16
13583 Berlin
florianwendland@freenet.de

Abstract

This article discusses the generic Java Emitter Templates 2 (JET2) template engine, with the focal point of its extensible capabilities to achieve a flexible customization of the whole model-to-text transformation process using JET2. Therefore, its internal workflows engine will be explored first, just as the process rules for Ecore based input models.

Based on this fundamental knowledge, the extension mechanism of JET2 will be presented to achieve a common understanding, of how a JET2 template engine internally works. Afterwards, we will demonstrate simple auxiliary functions via XPath to compute the full qualified name of a model element and via XML to generate the signature of even complex operations, modeled with UML2. In this step, a proposal for a flexible and maintainable development of extension will be presented. Considerations about the convenient testing of JET2 extensions complete this article.

In the end, a conclusion will summarize the elaborated aspects.

1 Introduction

Model-to-Text-Transformations seem to be straight forward, since they often translate model elements into text in a bidirectional manner. Of course they are, but they are also quite complex and, nevertheless, a crucial part of a model based development approach, which should be planed and implemented carefully. A transformation engine had to be integrated into a specific development process with a less of configuration issues and a lot of efficiency, because development time is a cost-intensive procedure.

The more complex a model driven approach is, the merrier a template engine had to fit its requirements. Some of the main features are: Traceability, to keep track of the transformation output to its input; scalability, to be able to process a growing number of model elements; protected regions, to mark some parts of the code as "unchangeable", so that a regenerated code keeps the code of the region during the generation process (this has been very well discussed in [3] and [4]); maintainability, to keep the templates clean and understandable for further improvements or bug fixings. These are just few points, which had to be considered, before a specific template engines will be chosen. Often, a single template engine will not fit all of these requirements or the desires, a developer had.

A template engine, which provides a convenient und intuitive extension mechanism, offers the possibility to upgrade the missing (or proprietary) functionality manually, and therefore, being very flexible to fit into nearly any scenario, a developer wants it to. The Jave Emitter Templates 2 (JET2) is such an extensible template engine. Its internal workflow engine is based on XML to control and execute the whole transformation process. Especially the uncomfortable access through UML was a great annoyance of the former Java Emitter Templates 1, where it was recommended by the developer community to map a complex UML model instance by an additional, may be error-prone transformation into a more abstract, yet simplified proprietary model. JET2 eliminates this inefficient creation of an intermediate model by providing both a very structured and readable template language and an XPath based access to any input model, whatever structure the model contains. The focal point of this paper lies on the architecture and the implementation of customized JET2 transformation functionality via XPath functions and XML elements to show, how JET2 can be used for proprietary problems and solutions.

2 Related Work

Model-to-Text-Transformations had been very well discussed in the last years. A general overview over the code generation in a MDA approach can be found in [1] and [2], which doesn't point out a specific template engine yet requirements model-to-text transformations had to realize.

A more concrete requirements analysis for model-to-text transformations had been done in [3] and [4]. The latter one introduces two code generation engines, which are used in an example process, namely genuaModel2Text-Transformator and the Java Emitter Templates 1.

Finally, [5] focuses a detailed description about the principles of code generating mechanisms and its capabilities. It also introduces the template engine Xpand, which is part of the openArchitectureWare [6] toolset.

3 Exploring JET2

3.1 Fundamentals

The Java Emitter Templates 2 (JET2) is a flexible, yet powerful template engine, which is able to process heterogeneous input models and to create textual artifacts out of them. JET2 accesses a generic input model elements via XPath location steps. Therefore, it implements the XPath 1.0 recommendation of the W3C [7] with some minor exceptions. Hence, JET2 needs an input model that is internally based on (or mapped by the modelloader to) a tree structure. This implies that JET2 templates are in principal powerful enough to transform various kinds of models like DOM or, for example, Ecore models.

JET2 fits to the requirements of a model driven approach since it is able to process

Ecore models out of the box, although its initial modelloader is defined for XML. But if a template engine wants to be a participant in a model driven toolrepository, it is mandatory to offer a convenient access to (mostly UML [8]) models.

3.1.1 Process Rules

Due to the fact, that the API of a model is abstracted by the surrounding XPath expression, a developer had to know the process rules of a modelloader. These rules are depending on both, the kinds and numbers of information sources of the input model and after the developer's fancy, who defines the mapping inside the modelloader. For Ecore models, these process rules are defined as follows:

- The root location path / is mapped to the underlying resource of the model. Hence, /contents is mapped to the procedure call resource.getContents().

- Node tests are realized for the selection of an EClass with equivalent name attribute. Although, it is possible to use a qualified name for the node test or a default XPath node test. It is even feasible to include complex predicates or built-in XPath-Functions into your location step, in order to express a more qualified, powerful selection. The expression /contents/Package returns a node set with all packages, that are directly contained by the resource, where /contents/node() returns a node set with any model element contained.

- XPath-Attributes (@qname) are shortcuts for a homonymous getter in the model element's API, so they are accessors for the corresponding attribute. /contents/Package[1]/@name returns the name of the first package of the resource.

- EReferences are treated like ordinary model elements, but beginning with a lower case instead of an upper one. Property/type/@name references the TypedElement of a Property and retrieves its name, if it exists.

These are the foundational process rules for any model, which depends on the Eclipse Modeling Framework [9], like the UML2-Project [10], which provides a full implementation of the UML2 metamodel.

3.1.2 Limitations of XPath

XML consists of only two metaelements: element and attribute, which are used by JET2 to map an location path to the information sources of the input model. This implies that only two kinds of information types are selectable. As we mentioned in subsection 1.1.3, XML elements are mapped to EClasses (or EReferences) and XML attributes to the corresponding attributes of the metaclass. In case the input model is an UML2 model, navigation is being done on UML2 metamodel layer (M2), not on Ecore layer (M3). There are situations in a transformation process, where it is crucial to access the metaclass of a model element instead of the element itself. Or imagine, the modeler had defined some stereotypes for the model, which should be transformed into special code artifacts. But how to select and process these additional information sources, which have no relations in XML? The answer is short and dissatisfying: there's no way! But this is not as worth as it could be, because JET2 provides a highly extensible architecture, that mitigates the lack of "built-in" information source access.

3.2. Architecture

JET2 is an Eclipse project, so it is not surprisingly, that its internal architecture is tailored into several bundles, each of them satisfying a dedicated requirement. The main capability of the JET2 core bundle is to establish a generic process model by declaring some extension points for concrete implementations and glue all the registered implementation together for integrative usage. Figure 1 visualizes a simplified architectural view of JET2 as an customized UML component diagram.

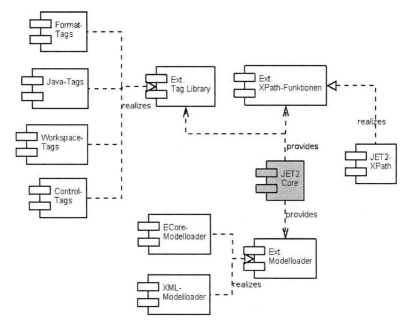

Figure 1: An architectural overview of JET2

3.2.1.Templates

Templates are the main artifacts within JET2, since they define the behavior of the transformation process in a declarative way. JET2 accomplishes the code generation process in an indirect way, separated into two gradual steps.

1. Translation: Each template declaration is parsed and compiled into executable Java sources.

2. Generation: The Java sources are instantiated and invoked from the JET2 runtime to produce the desired artifacts.

When a new JET2 project is created, it seems that the XML templates are being directly invoked by the engine. This is a factual error, because all instructions and XPath location steps are just declarative statements, which abstract the underlying implementation. Figure 2 shows the internal translation and invocation mechanism of JET2.

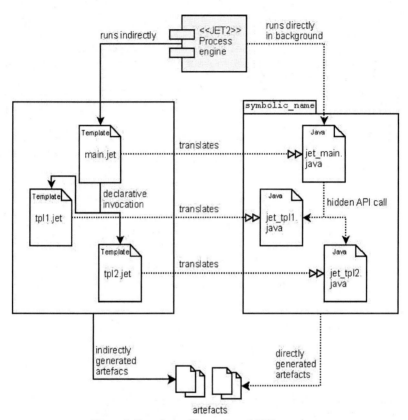

Figure 2: Translation/Generation of JET2 templates

By default, the translated Java sources are hidden in the Eclipse Package Explorer. This can be deactivated through the Package Explorer's filter settings. It is not feasible to manipulate the generated sources manually, since they will be regenerated, every time the developer saves the template. However, the integration of the prototypical JET2 editor is not as stable as other Eclipse editors are, so that it is sometimes necessary to resolve some runtime errors by hand, for example missing import statements.

3.2.2.TagLibraries

The built-in Tag Libraries are tailored into four different flavors, each of them with a specific intention:

- **org.eclipse.jet.controlTags:** Control Tags are the elementary control instructions, which configure the process flow inside the templates. The library summarizes important tags for element access, iterating over a node set by a loop or invoking other templates, to produce the desired output.
- **org.eclipse.jet.formatTags:** Format Tags offer occasional needed auxiliary functions like UUID generation or date/time formatting.
- **org.eclipse.jet.workspaceTags:** Workspace Tags manipulate the Eclipse workspace, thus they are predetermined for the creation of project, folders, files from within a transformation process.
- **org.eclipse.jet.javaTags:** JET1 is the template engine of the Eclipse Modeling Framework, where it generates the Java based model implementation. It is imaginable, that JET1 will be replaced in near (or far) future EMF distributions by JET2, so there are some built-in tags for Java code generation in particular. It defines needful functionality to resolve cumbersome constructs, for example a convenient mechanism (via java:importsLocation) for the arrangement of import statements. In Java, the imports had to be declared in the file header, but in a straight forward process the cross-package imports are collected during the resolution/generation of constructs like attributes and/or operation bodies, deep inside a class structure.

3.2.2.XPath-Functions

In addition to the built-in functions of the XPath 1.0 recommendation, JET2 provides some extra functionality, which basically operates on the manipulation of string literals.

The Java coding convention, that operations and attributes should begin with a lower case and compose different word parts in a so called „camel case" style, demanded a perseverative computation algorithm. This algorithm is outsourced to the default XPath-Function „camelCase", which requires a whitespace separated list of word parts. The expression <c:get select="camelCase(„get Model Driven Approach")"/> generates get-ModelDrivenApproach in the output artifact.

Needless to say, because of the implementation of the XPath 1.0 recommendation, all the XPath concepts like node axis, node tests, predicates or built-in functions within a JET2 template are available.

3.2.3.Modelloader

Modelloader are essential for any transformation process. They configure how an abstract XPath location step is mapped to the concrete model representation. They are especially responsible for the loading mechanism. It is imaginable, to implement a modelloader for remote models like databases or even a modelloader, that processes an AST of a programming language. Modelloaders contain the most brainpower, because they define the fundamental access to the input model.

A template developer is rarely encountered with implementation details of a modelloader, since everything, that is concerned with calling the API of the modelloader (or even of the model) is done in the background by the translated Java source representation of the template.

3.3 Deploying and running a JET2 transformation

JET2 transformations are exported and deployed as ordinary Eclipse plugins via the export capability of the IDE. Once a JET2 project is available in the plugin registry, one can invoke the process by using either the run configuration wizard or calling the API dynamically from within a third party plugin. The dynamic invocation capability opens JET2 to be included into any Eclipse application.

4 Extensions to JET2

One of the most powerful capabilities of JET2 is its extensible architecture. Nearly every core concept, on which the JET2 transformation engine is based, can be customized, including XPath-Functions, Tag Libraries and Modelloader. Only the first both concepts are discussed, due to the shortage of space.

4.1. Individual XPath-Functions

XPath-Functions are intended for being used inside location steps or to do some computation with a given node set. They are realizations of the extension point org.eclipse.jet.xpathFunctions, where the minimum and maximum number of parameters and a concrete implementation class had to be declared. XPath-Functions return always a value. Implementations are instances of the org.eclipse.jet.xpath.XPathFunction interface.

Let's assume, we want to compute the qualified name of a class/interface, for example for cross-package communication within the system. Each packageable element in the UML metamodel contains a derived attribute qualifiedName, that returns the qualified name of the context element, separated by a double-colon (package1::package2::Class). In Java, namespaces are spanned by a dot separated syntax (package1.package.Class). One solution might be to define a XPath-Function which handles this with two parameters. The first one is the package, which contains the context object in the model, the second one is the separating string literal. Figure 3 shows one possible implementation.

```
1    public class ComputeQualifiedName extends AbstractXPathFunction{
2        public Object evaluate(List args){
3            final Package _package = (Package)args.get(0);
4            final String sep = XPathUtil.xpathString(args.get(1));
5            return
UMLUtilities.recursivePackageName(_package,"",sep);
6        }
7    }
```

Figure 3: XPath-Function that resolves the qualified name of a model element

Parameters passed to a XPath-Function are summed up in a generic List object, thus, the parameter need to be casted into the desired and correct type. In this case, the objects are casted without a preceding check against their actual types (via the instanceof-Operator).

XPathUtil is a utility class provided by the org.eclipse.jet plugin. It publics only a very few, less complicated operations, commonly for casting the parameters to primitive types. UMLUtilities are part of another utility plugin, which encapsulates the access to the UML2 API. We will discuss the reason for outsourcing this functionality later.

The function can be called from within any position in the templates, where a function call is possible. Commonly, this is used for assigning values to attributes or variables.

4.2. Customizing Tag Libraries

4.2.1. Different types of tags

JET2 knows different types of tags, which can be implemented. They differ mainly in the way of internal processing its content and parameter passing mechanism.

- Conditional tags: They evaluate a conditional expression to a boolean result. If it evaluates to true, the process engine is allowed to process the content, that is surround by the conditional tags. The <c:if>-statement in the ControlTag library is a representative of a conditional tag. The name of the attribute, containing the conditional expression is not fixed to @test, even if the XPath recommendation does it in this way.

- Function tags: Function tags are commonly the most used tags in a transformation, because it is their part to write content out to the artifacts. Their input is determined from both their contents and their dedicated attributes. Functional tags have methods, which execute either before or after the content was processed. Since these tags are instances of the generic ContainerTag interface, a functional tag expressed as <anEmptyFunction /> will never produce any output.

- Iteration tags: Iteration tags are recommended for creating some kinds of loops for a special requirement. By default, JET2 provides the <c:iterate> function, that traverses a node set by a given location path. Since this is a forward loop, it is imaginable to implement a loop, which first inverses the node set and afterwards iterate obviously reverse over the set.

- Empty Tags: Empty Tags are the simplest tag types, the only consist of attributes, which are pulled up for the computation of the output.

4.2.2. An implementation example

In a model-to-code transformation, it is often desired to compute the signature of an operation of an UML class. UML classes are commonly converted to classes of the programming language (if the target language is an object oriented one). This sounds very

141

easy, but a developer had to consider about several computational things: the visibility, the return type, the formal parameters, cardinality of the parameters and return type, etc. Directly included in the template, this may pollute the template code with a lot of element accesses, which are quite intuitive but tedious. It might ease the whole process, if there would be a dedicated tag which takes the responsibility for this computation. Figure 3 shows, how a possible implementation could be realized by implementing the empty tag extension point.

Empty tags must implement the `EmptyTag` interface, that publics the method `doAction(TagInfo, JET2Context, JET2Writer)`. TagInfo contains meta information about the occurrence of the tag in the template; JET2Context wraps the execution environment of the transformation process; JET2Writer is a decorator interface for JET2 specific content writing. One can register an `IWriterListener` at the JET2Writer, which will be informed when

a) the writer finalizes the output buffer and is ready to write the content to the artifact via `IWriterListener.finalizeContent(JET2Writer, Object)`,

b) the writer has already written the content to the artifact via `IWriterListener.postCommitContent(JET2Writer, Object)`.

From inside a template, the function will be invoked with `<xyz:computeOperationSignatur operation="op"/>`, where @op is the name of the variable containing the UML operation element. Mostly, empty tags can be realized also as XPath-Functions and vice versa.

```
1    public class GenerateOperationName extends AbstractEmptyTag {
2    public void doAction(TagInfo td, JET2Context context,
     JET2Writer out) throws    JET2TagException {
3        final Operation op = (Operation)
         context.getVariable( td.getAttribute("operation"));
4        final StringBuffer buf = new StringBuffer();
5        buf.append(op.getVisibility().getLiteral());
6        buf.append(' ');
7        if(op.isStatic()){
8            buf.append("static ");
9        }
10       final Parameter returnType =
         UMLUtilities.getReturnType( op.getOwnedParameters());
11       if(returnType != null){
12           buf.append(UMLUtilities.resolveCardinality
             (returnType));
13       }else{
14           buf.append("void");
15       }
16       buf.append(' ');
17       buf.append(op.getName());
18       buf.append("(");
19       buf.append(UMLUtilities.computeFormalParameter
         ( op.getOwnedParameters()));
```

142

```
20        buf.append(")");
21        out.write(buf.toString());
22        }
23   }
```

Figure 4: Empty Tag implementation that computes an operation signature

4.3 Extensible Architecture

To achieve a reusable and cycle-free extension architecture, the distribution of the plugins had to be sensibly accomplished. In section 2.1. and 2.2., we made use of an external utility class, in fact UMLUtilities. It is included in a separate plugin, which exhibits no dependencies to any JET2 mechanisms. Therefore, it might be included in different scenarios and/or by several template engines, which are integrated in the Eclipse environment. See Figure 5 for more details.

5. Testing

Delivering untested, may be erroneous software is a quite unreliable proceeding. Every kind of software should be thoroughly tested, before it will be amenable to a (hopefully) widespread number of users. This also applies to JET2 transformation definitions too.

Unfortunately, it's impossible to test an extension within the same Eclipse instance, where it was developed during the development process. This belongs to internal implementation details of JET2. So, one had to repeat the time intensive deploying procedure each time, the extension was changed. Even with an automatic built script, is this an highly inefficient step. But, fortunately, Eclipse offers a way, to mitigate the impractical (at least for testing) deployment structure of JET2.

The extensions can be tested as a JUnit Plug-in Test. In such a test, all the plugins, specified in the test configuration wizard, are included for the JUnit test environment. This enables us to implement a simple test method in each extension class and to setup the execution environment. It has to be said, that setting up a test execution environment for Tag Libraries can be complicated, because one had to create the JET2 environment and all of its context object, that are necessary for a real simulation. However, XPath-Functions are much easier and efficient to test by creating just the needed input and calling the evaluate() method directly. This depends on the nature of XPath, where access to the JET2 environment is not mandatory.

6. Conclusion

With JET2, a developer has a widespread set of predefined functions and a well structured process engine available to create generic, maintainable, extensible and modular structured model-to-code transformation projects. The concrete model is abstracted by XPath expressions, which are mapped to the model API by the JET2 runtime engine using a modelloader and a modelinspector. (The latter was not focused in this article, but for completeness he should be mentioned anyway.)

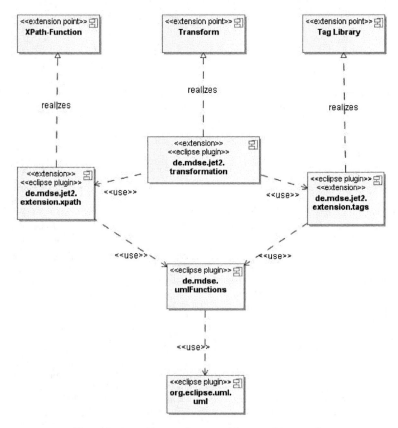

Figure 5: An architectural proposal for reusable extensions

We have seen, how the evidential limitations of JET2 concerning the gathering of data from more than two information sources of a model element, can erased by providing the desired functionality by custom extensions.

It would be interesting to examine JET2 in a more sophisticated (business) project with real requirements and models. It is the author's opinion, that in particular of the intuitive XPath localization, JET2 may fit into a great numbers of real world scenarios, with less development effort and a gain of both, time and money.

Bibliography

[1] Kleppe, Anneke; Warmer, Jos; Bast, Wim: MDA Explained: the model driven architecture: practice and promise. Pearson Education Inc., 2003. ISBN 0-321-19442-X.

[2] Mellor, Stephen J.; Scott, Kendall; Uhl, Axel; Wiese, Dirk: MDA Distilled: principles of model driven architecture. Pearson Education Inc., 2004. ISBN 0-201-78891-8

[3] Petrasch, Roland; Meimberg, Oliver: Model Driven Architecture. Dpunkt-Verlag Heidelberg, 2006. ISBN: 978-3-89864-343-6

[4] Gruhn, Volker; Pieper, Daniel; Röttgers, Carsten: MDA. Springer-Verlag Berlin Heidelberg, 2006. ISBN: 978-3-540-28744-5

[5] Stahl, Thomas; Völter, Markus; Efftinge, Sven; Haase, Arno: Modellgetriebene Softwareentwicklung: Techniken, Engineering, Management. Dpunkt-Verlag Heidelberg, 2007. ISBN: 978-3-89864-448-8

[6] openArchitectureWare: openArchitectureWare Homepage, oAW.org. http://www.openarchitectureware.org.

[7] XPath 1.0 Specification: XPath 1.0 Recommendation, World Wide Web Consortium (W3C). http://www.w3.org/TR/xpath.

[8] UML Specifications: UML Superstructure and Infrastructure, Object Management Group (OMG). http://www.omg.org/spec/UML/2.1.2/.

[9] EMF Project: Eclipse Modeling Framework Project (EMF), Eclipse Foundation http://www.eclipse.org/modeling/emf.

[10] UML2 Project: UML2-Project (MDT-UML2), Eclipse Foundation http://www.eclipse.org/modeling/mdt/?project=uml2#uml2.